There Is Life After Drugs –

How Bad Do You Want It?

There Is Life After Drugs –
How Bad Do You Want It?

Pastor Ray Houston

Copyright © 2010 by Pastor Ray Houston

Library of Congress Control Number: 2010908768

ISBN: Hardcover   978-0-9831946-0-6
          Paperback   978-0-9831946-1-3
          E-Book   978-0-9831946-2-0

All rights reserved. No part of this book may be reproduced or transmitted in any form or by any means, electronic or mechanical, including photocopying, recording, or by any information storage and retrieval system, without permission in writing from the copyright owner.

Disclaimer: If in this book I come across as the lover, the player or the cool guy I know and understand and therefore must let you know that at my best I was really only Ghetto-Fabulous.

Disclaimer: If to anyone that is mention in this book or anyone reading this book I sound derogatory or offensive remember this is my story and my reflection of how I felt things were. It may not reflect the opinions or reflections of others.

This book was printed in the United States of America.

Printed by :   Lightning Source
                La Vergne, TN

To order additional copies of this book, contact:

Publisher: Daddy's Girl Promotions, LLC
             5208 Merrick Drive • Peachtree City, GA 30269
             (708) 351-2581

     You may also order online at Barnes & Noble and Amazon

Visit us on the Web:
www.daddysgirlspromotions.com
Email: pastorray@pastorrayhouston.com

Contents

Chapter One	The Beginning	9
Chapter Two	Altering of the Mind	47
Chapter Three	Desire and Control	55
Chapter Four	Root Problems	61
Chapter Five	Owning Up to "Satan Is Pimping Me"	69
Chapter Six	The Enabler	73
Chapter Seven	Caught Up the Hard Place	81
Chapter Eight	The Art of Effective Ministry	85
Pastor Ray		101
Index		103

Dedications

To the memory of my late parents, Mr. Kazie and Mrs. Henrie Mae Houston, for always teaching me the truth.

To my oldest daughter and son, Neoccesha and Nicky, whom I loved always but let down in my addiction. I am thankful that you let me back into your lives.

To my baby daughter, Cheriamor—I must dedicate this book to you also because you as well as Neoccesha and Nicky have been my inspiration and true sign of strength.

To, the late Reverend James C. Carpenter, Sr., my pastor forever, a pastor with true ministry at heart.

To Pastor O. C. Gibson, a lasting and true friend, and Mother Cornelia Burns, a real prayer warrior in ministry and a friend whose friendship is beyond words.

To my mentors, the late Reverend Don Pagel and Pastor Thomas Barclay.

To Wendy, a.k.a. Monya Nelson, for being a true friend, especially during the loss of my mother even after I had not been a true friend. What a friend.

To Marie Glover, thank you for being the sanity for me during an insane time in my life. You are a great friend.

To our good friends Pastors Al and Geri Young. How would I have made it without you?

And last but not least, to my wife, Colleen, without whom this book would have never happened. I love you.

Chapter One

The Beginning

Although I was on drugs for nineteen years before my last baby was born, I didn't get hooked on the pipe until after I got custody of Cheriamor when she was about two years old. Just before I got my baby, I was living in a hotel in downtown Milwaukee. I was running my construction company and living a lie, believing that it was going to get back to where it had been in 1982. The year was 1986, and I was only dreaming. I was capable but not living in reality. Like always, I was making money but not using it right. My dream was that of being a successful businessman, of becoming a conglomerate, if you will, able to help people all around the world. I wanted to provide homes, have my own schools, and create jobs for all those who wanted a better life. I had grown up in Milwaukee in the fifties in the poorest part of town until 1966 when I turned fourteen, and we moved to a better part of the inner city. I suppose I dreamed so big because we lived so low. When Cheriamor was born, I didn't realize how much I had stopped living any type of meaningful life although I still had big dreams, but in reality, now my life was all about women, weed, and wine.

I got Cheriamor, who we nicknamed ReRe, around June of 1986. I had gone over to her mother's house to see the baby and bring her some needed supplies as my usual custom was. When I got there, I knocked on the door, but there was no answer. I thought I heard crying, so I started banging on the door, but still no answer. Sure now that I heard loud crying, I turned the knob, and the door was open. Entering the house, I ran up the stairs and into the apartment. There was my baby in her crib by herself, crying hysterically. Dirty and nasty with a faded white T-shirt on and a nasty diaper that had crap in it. She reached for me through her little tears. My heart melted. I grabbed my baby, wiped her little face, took that stinky diaper and faded T-shirt off, and walked out of the house with her butt naked. I never looked back. Her mother's version was that she had left ReRe with a babysitter, who had stepped out just for a moment and I just came in and stole her. I later went to court and got custody of my daughter. However, my sister kept her until our mother died in December 1986. Every day, I was there spending time with her, but I didn't keep her overnight until December 1986. During the day, you would find me spending time with Neocessha, Nicky (my other two children who lived with their mother), and Cheriamor; and at nighttime, I spent time with the women, the weed, and the wine.

Right after my mother died, my sister gave ReRe to me and told me I had to take care of her myself. I told her Mama had just died and I just wasn't up to it yet, but she said, "Yeah, my mama just died too, so I know how you feel." As I stated before, I was doing construction and living in a hotel in downtown Milwaukee. I didn't want to bring ReRe there. My sister, Mattie, told me she felt I should move in with my dad, help him, and be there for him. She meant well, but this was the worst thing for all of us because of how I was spending my money or, should I say, wasting my money. I didn't have any cash on hand to just run out and get an apartment. My dad was seventy-two years old, and surely, he didn't need my help or a seventeen-month-old granddaughter terrorizing his house. The last thing I needed was to be back in the old neighborhood where I had lived as a kid. I had moved downtown because no one knew me there and I could stay away from the pipe, which was taking over the inner city. This move put me right back around the people that didn't want anything and weren't going anywhere (a lot of them anyway). I may not have been living right by night, but I wanted something, had gotten something; and even though I had lost it, I believed I could get it again.

I really wanted something from life. Most of those around me in my old neighborhood had laughed at me when I was working as an apprentice in the painter's union trying to get my degree so I could go into business for myself. As a matter of fact, many in my old neighborhood were always laughing, calling me the hardest-working man in town. When I got my business up and running, I had compassion and gave some of them jobs. I also helped a few family members who had hung out in the neighborhood all their lives and were now in their twenties and down on their luck. A part of my fall in business was my own doing, but about 50 percent of it was because of some of the people that I tried to help. They turned around and did me so wrong, so very wrong, while working for me. They just didn't seem to care, but then jealously is crueler than the grave (Song of Solomon 8:6).

So here I was back in my old hood, around a lot of people, not all, but a lot of who could be called the cool, the crude, and the carefree. I would have rather lived next door to hell. Here I was, thirty-five years old, a single parent living back at home in the old hood with my dad. Before this, for about two years, I had lived with my other two children and their mother in one of the houses I owned. That was between 1978 and 1980. Even though I had two homes, I chose to live in downtown Milwaukee. That afforded me the opportunity to do what I wanted. I went to work, I came home, and then I went where I wanted to without question. I could stay out all night or have someone stay half the night. I spent time with Neoccesha and Nicky every day and gave them money. I went to church and other places, always being around in the daytime, but at night I took them to my mother, who lived next door to their mother. From 1972 until 1986, I had never kept any of my kids overnight by myself. Nightlife belonged to me. It was on December 20, 1986, that I gave up my room at the hotel and moved back to the old house in the old neighborhood. On December 21, I got up early, took ReRe to day care, and got to work thirty miles away by 6:45 a.m. I cursed everybody and everything for thirty miles.

While I was at work, I started thinking that maybe I needed a wife. I cried for "forty days and forty nights." Through the tears I made bottles, changed Pampers, ironed little dresses, and braided little hair. At the thought of needing a wife and settling down, I got even better at the single-parenting thing.

Because of how I met ReRe's mom and the type of relationship we had, life with my baby had a rocky start. ReRe was six weeks old by the time I'd seen her for the first time; the fact of not knowing if I was the father for sure before she was born had made our beginning difficult. I found having a baby daughter and being back at home made me so very unhappy. Women didn't ask me over as much because they didn't want me to bring my baby. They wanted me to be free (well, you know why), and most of the time, I couldn't get a babysitter. Now I found that I had to deal with real women and leave the easy party girls behind. Parenthood was ruining my sin life. Sitting around the house all evening after working all day, I became evil and hateful. I had lost my joy while trying to become a loving dad. I was back in church trying to live saved, but there was not any joy in my life. Evilness and hatefulness, the devil's twins, jumped joy and beat him almost to death. The party girls were gone, and most women that I met wanted a single man who was free to take care of them and their kids. So I didn't have joy because I didn't have the women, and those twins, evilness and hatefulness, would not let me go. I had always found joy in something or somebody, and it was always worldly. I had never learned to have joy in loving God because at the time, I didn't know him for real. I wasn't yet able to love being a parent because it was so demanding. My other two kids were right next door. I had to spend time with them and the baby and then work. I was busy chasing ReRe under the table and behind the sofa and getting her from under the bed. She didn't go to sleep until two thirty in the morning, which kept me awake. Neoccesha and Nicky thought ReRe was some kind of doll that they could play with and pump full of candy, and then they went home to do their homework, leaving me and their seventy-three-year-old granddad with a hyped-up two-year-old full of candy.

I found myself falling. I tried to run, but I ran too slow and too late. With evilness, hatefulness, and now loneliness holding me down, the pipe was finally able to overtake me. It got me. This was the beginning of my fall. I started using the pipe before I met Marie but had not gotten addicted yet. I was still functional, but it wouldn't be long before desire would turn to control. I always teach that when you have no joy, no peace, and no focus, you are no match for the devil or his vices because if you lose just one of these, imagine how horrible life could become, but if you lose all three, can you image how horrific life will become?

So on October 4, 1987, evilness, hatefulness, and loneliness held me down and took a pipe and put it in my mouth. I spent $2,695 within forty-eight hours. From March 1978 until November 6, 1987, I always had three or four thousand dollars stashed somewhere. Although I had been a drinker, smoked weed, snorted coke, used heroine, and whatever else, I always had a good amount of money around; but even as I write this book, I realize that I have no bragging rights to say that I always had three or four thousand dollars at any given time. Without the women, the weed, and the wine, I should have had about sixty thousand dollars in the bank and about six to eight thousand dollars hidden in my secret stash. Now I was broke from 1987 until January 20, 1995. People say you don't miss something worth something until you lose it.

I continued to work hard at being a single parent. People were always complimenting me, saying, "Everywhere you go, you have your baby with you." She was now around two and a half, and there were no more Pampers. Hallelujah! Things had gotten better. I had gotten to the place where I could at least say that I had learned how to be a good single parent. My kids came first, at least in my mind. I now took pride in being that single dad. It was hard, but I was getting better. I felt good about how far I had come—from playboy to parent in less than a year. I even had a real woman in my life that really loved me.

I met Marie while working on a project in Milwaukee. She had been working at this place for about ten years. Maria had been divorced for about seven years. She had three children ages nineteen, seventeen, and fourteen. Now get this, the only man she had been with in her life was her husband. I was changing. After a few conversations with her while I was going in and out of the building, she finally gave me her phone number. I started going by her house to visit, and after a while, we started dating. Yep, Marie was a real woman, a wonderful woman. She was doing all she could to help me keep the mind-set of loving the responsibility of being a parent. She was great with her children and with ReRe. I tried to hold on to the new me and my new relationship, which was not sexual, and I wasn't seeing anyone on the side. Yep, I was changing.

Although I had tried the pipe as I mentioned before, I was fighting back and holding on. I didn't really understand I was in the fight of my life, for my life. Marie and I were both in church, and I was, for the first time in my life, admitting to her and others that I felt I was called to be a pastor. I was happy for the first time since I lost my childhood sweetheart in 1970. Although my childhood sweetheart and I got back together and had two children, I was never happy again until now. Now sixteen years and two million dollars later, I was able to say to a woman that I loved her, I trusted her, and I wanted to get married to her. I tried so hard to hold on to the new way I felt about life, about being a real parent, and being in a real relationship. I now realize I wanted to be more than a single parent. I wanted to be a family. I had lost that hope in 1970 when I lost my childhood sweetheart, but now it seemed possible again.

The Beginning

I remember that as far back as junior high school, I was always dreaming about being a husband and a father just like my dad. That had meant more to me than one day playing football or running track. The two million dollars I made as a businessman from 1976 to 1984 gave me no joy because I didn't have anyone to believe in and no one to be a family with. I met Marie three heartbeats before October 4, before the pipe. She seemed to be a spark of sanity in the midst of my insanity. I wanted so much what seemed to make me whole, the ideal of love, getting married for the first time, having the love of Neoccesha and Nicky, and sharing the love I had for them. Then ReRe—all she had to take care of her was me, her dad.

I really tried to give my little girl a "mother's love" because next to the love of Jesus, there is no greater love than a mother's love. I could not do it as Ray, but from the day I got ReRe, I knew I had to find a way to give her that mother's love. I tried so hard to hold on. I know it may sound hypocritical to say I have always been in the church with all the things I say I have done in my life, but it's the truth. I was always in the church, but for the first time in life, I was seeking God for real. I promised God I would give up women, weed, and wine if He would help me not to lose my baby girl over drugs. See, I was scared because although I was seeing Marie and it wasn't a sexual relationship, I was still a coldhearted player deep at heart. Even though I wanted to be different, even though I wanted to change, I was the epitome of the old saying "It is hard for a leopard to change its spots."

For example, in 1982, I had planned on just leaving Milwaukee, my family, and my business and head to the West Coast. I was not going there to be a contractor. I believed I was at the top of my game as a player. I was going to live off the ladies, but God had other plans. The day I put a down payment on my Mercedes was the day I found out that the person I was planning on having something really bad done to because of some dirt he had done to me, had a hit put on him by someone else. In their attempt to take him out, another person got killed. Guess who people were looking at for the hit? Because of the bad blood between us, most people thought I did it. Although suspected, I dodged that bullet; but before I could get out of town, I got hit with sixteen felonies. These I was guilty of.

I made God all kinds of promises if He would just help me not go to jail. I walked into the federal court guilty and told the truth and why I did it. However, because of the nature of the felonies and what went down, I cannot tell you who caused me to do the crimes. For some reason, God answered this sinner's prayer. I walked out of the courthouse without any felonies, just one misdemeanor and two hundred hours of community service, and they took $50,000 from moneys I had coming to me. But now it's 1987, five years later, and I had not kept my promises to God. This wasn't the first miracle God had shown me. He had worked three other miracles in my life prior, and I had failed Him. Thank God for His twins, grace and mercy.

On October 14, 1987, I was on the phone telling someone, "I can stop smoking the pipe whenever I want 'cause all I have to do is get right with God, and I know He will bring me out. I just don't want to stop right now because I am loving this thang." But I was just fooling myself because as much as I wanted to really hold on to the new me for the sake of my kids and Marie and the possibility of having a real family, it was not enough to keep me from the long journey of addiction I was headed for. I thought I wanted this new life as much as I had wanted to be like Fredrick Douglass, Malcolm X, and Dr. King. I felt I wanted this new family as much as I wanted to be like Babe Ruth, Jim Brown, and Hank Aaron, but as usual, things in my perfect world did not line up with things in my real world. In my real world, I went through the painter's union as an apprentice to become a journeyman. I had to work like a dog sometimes, being on ladders as high as forty feet in the air, but I did it because I dreamed in my perfect world of having a successful business. But in my real world, I started my own little company at the bottom of the barrel, at the lowest end.

I went into business before I was ready because I wasn't picked up by a union company during the spring of 1976. The first two years of business were pure hell, but then things changed during the spring of 1978. My first two years I had done forty thousand dollars in business. During 1978, I did $250,000 in business, and by December 1982, I had done almost two million dollars worth of business. That's pretty good for a poor boy from the poorest part of town who started his first day of business with only two dollars in his pocket that his mama gave him to buy some bologna and crackers for lunch. We didn't have a van, so my partner and I carried the ladders on our backs to the job.

Now in the real world, the felonies of 1982 took everything from me. I didn't go to jail, but I had nothing. I lost two homes, seven trucks, my car, sixteen workers, fifty thousand dollars, and I was banned from doing federal work for one year. I remember praying and asking God to take my life 'cause I didn't want to live without my money, my women, and my possessions. But God would not let me off that easy, so through prayer, seeking God, and perseverance, I rallied back to start all over again, but now all I had fought for combined didn't concern me as much as wanting to smoke that damned pipe. My real world, controlled by the addiction, was greater than the business I had fought for or the family I wanted in my perfect world. Now I just wanted to get high. I didn't even take my business seriously any longer. I would hire myself out as some type of subcontractor. I made great money for the dope man. I no longer spent money on Cheriamor. Gone were the shopping sprees for her. The clothes she had she continued to wear even though she had outgrown them.

Mattie and Marie were now buying things for my baby because I always had some great lie about what I was doing with my money in the business.

Marie had bought me a new car, and she was driving my old one. She only wanted ReRe and me to have the best, but now her love and affection didn't mean anything to me; nothing did. All I cared about, all I lived for, was Friday, for the high. Gone were the evenings of playing on the floor with my baby. Even though I stayed at home Sunday through Friday afternoon because I had spent all my money, we did nothing. I sat on the sofa every evening after work waiting for payday Friday. I didn't rob or try to hustle to get money. No, like a fool, I just worked hard all week long and paid the dope man on the weekend. I was no longer helping my dad with the bills, the food, or anything else.

When asked about why I didn't have any money, I always told people I was waiting for a payment. I never had anything to say, nothing to talk about. I just wanted Friday to hurry up and come. I lived for the weekend. I tried to fake it with Marie, but I couldn't. I had been so upbeat when we first met. I always talked about God, my kids, her and her kids, and the granddaughter she was raising. I talked about family, the business, and all the things we could do together, but now I was always so far away, so very distant. She tried to do more to make me happy. She was already keeping ReRe half the time after work, feeding both of us and spending most of the money when we did anything together. She really cared about ReRe and me. She did anything and everything she could for us. I knew she really loved us. She would always ask me what was wrong, and I would always come up with some lie. I talked with Marie while writing this book to let her know I was including her in it because she was such a big part of ReRe and my story, but I didn't tell her this part. Help me, Jesus! After a while, I started having sex in the smoke houses.

A smoke house is not like a dope house where you just come, buy your drugs, and leave. A smoke house is where people come to smoke their dope. Usually, men come with dope because they know women will be there waiting and willing to have sex for drugs. They know they could get a "dope date," if you will. A lot of times, women will catch a trick on the corner and bring him to the smoke house, where she can make the house money and they can use a room. Although I had been a lover and a player and had had all kinds of women and sexual experiences, the sex in a smoke house was so different. Listen to me! Run—no, the other way, the opposite way! As fast as you can. This experience is a big part of why so many can't leave the drugs alone. Most individuals in the smoke house will let their hair down like never before 'cause this is a part of what drugs make you want to do. You let the freak come out. I know I am going to get in trouble with the women here, but drugs will cause some women to go further than they could ever imagine, because what really goes on is that women get to do things they really already wanted to do but were too bashful or ashamed to do. But now they can blame it on the drugs and get paid for it. Men too! A lot of men who aren't good with the women make out great in the smoke house because they don't have to be fine or a great lover or go through all the formalities of taking the girl out to dinner or engaging her in great conversation. They just have to have dope, and the women in the smoke house will get freaky as the men want, no questions asked. They will be freaky as long as the men want as long as there are drugs. The freakiness and the whole atmosphere of the smoke house is part of what keeps men hooked, keeps them coming back, keeps them spending all their money. Here, they are allowed to be king for a day, dominant and in control—a man's fantasy.

Here, they have the ability to get what they want, when they want it, the way they want it because they have what the woman wants—drugs. I didn't know freaky until I got hooked on the pipe and started having sex with women on dope. Lord, have mercy on my soul. I won't own up to some of the things I did even at gunpoint. Shoot me! If this sounds appealing or intriguing to anyone, you are—excuse me—"a damned fool!" (Proverbs 1:7, 12:1, 15). Cheriamor and Marie would have had a better chance of taking on Kobe Bryant and LeBron James than me and that pipe.

By March 1988, Marie had had enough. The new car was damaged on every side. She had stopped seeing me as much because I wasn't even a shell of the man she had met. With tears in her eyes, she gave me the keys to my old car, asked for the keys to her new car, and asked me to please get out of her life. She said she would do anything for ReRe at any time, but she couldn't deal with my unexplainable, crazy madness anymore. Before the pipe, Marie was the person God had used to help me strive to be a good parent and start living again. I learned real fast that she had been my sanity.

For Cheriamor and me—well, our lives changed again really quickly from the day Marie walked out. My baby was now about to go through a nightmare like never before. Cheriamor and I moved out to our own hell, I mean place. Although I loved Marie—she was so good to me and seemed just right for me—I was not able to heal until I lost her. Jeremiah 18:1-12 and St. John 12:24 talks about this concept.

Back to being on our own, I got worse. ReRe only ate good when we went to visit someone. She never had enough to eat at home. Sometimes I had to go without eating just so she could eat. Our phone was usually always off, and the television was in pawn. She wore clothes that were always old and too little for her. If the rent got paid, it was never on time. I had been through hard times, but never like this. Mattie would have to pick ReRe up from day care sometimes because I hardly ever got there on time. Poor ReRe had to sit there some Fridays until almost five thirty without having anything to eat since noon, waiting for her daddy. But even then, not once did she ever not run up to me with joy and give me the biggest hug whenever I showed up. After about four months of this, I had had enough. I was sexed out, smoked out, and bombed out. Enough was enough! I had seen ReRe suffer enough. I had cared but not enough to want to stop until now.

Remember that phone call I said I made when I first got hooked on the pipe? The one where I said, "All I had to do is get right with God, and I knew He would bring me out"? Well, I will never ever, I mean never ever—no, for real—never ever take God for granted again! Lord God, have mercy on my crazy soul please, Jesus. Here I was hooked on the pipe, but I was in church every time the doors opened. I went out and got all kinds of Bibles. I prayed in tongues one day at work for eight hours and still ended up getting high on the way home. Oh God, help me, please! Now I wanted to stop. I wanted to be a parent again, but Satan had his claws sunk in real good.

I had learned a lot about me in the last year. I now was forced to come face-to-face with my selfish, unrealistic self. For the first time ever, I didn't feel God in my life. I felt like the person in Psalm 88, destitute, lost, and hopeless. ReRe was getting older. I no longer had a baby but a three-year-old. I was back to doing hair, ironing, and washing clothes, keeping house, and working every day. I was now living saved five and a half days a week. Although I was the same old junkie on the outside to most people, there was a new me forming on the inside. Slowly, I began to feel God again, but things didn't get any better yet; in fact, at this point, my addiction got worse. The worse my addiction got, the more I found myself seeking God.

The Word of God had become so real to me now because I had spent time studying from all kinds of study Bibles and textbooks. I no longer just believed in God because my mama raised me to believe in Him, but I had enough proof that God was real for myself. My faith, the archaeological findings, and much more had assured my faith and convinced my intellect. I read books from authors like Watchman Nee, Bill Bright, and others. I've seen where David and Eli were so very sad as parents, and I wanted to be the best parent I could be because that was part of what God expected in His Word. I wanted to be the parent of Proverbs 22:6 and train my child in the ways of God, but it seemed the more I desired to be a good parent and live for God, the more the evil one attacked me with my addiction.

This is one of Satan's favorite verses. Only he says, "Don't train up a child in the ways of God, and when they are older, they won't know which way to go." Although I was constantly in church, it seemed as though I would never get off drugs. But I was assured from talking with God that one day I would be free, but He wanted to know if I wanted it for real. Then He gave me what would become my battle cry throughout my life and throughout ministry—"How bad do you want it?" Because I took Him for granted, because I broke my other promises to Him, because of my disobedience, God allowed my addiction to linger until the love and need for drugs died. I wanted it gone now, but He still didn't take it away yet. He wanted to totally uproot it from me forever. I now hated drugs as much as I hated its master, Satan, but everything else got better except my drug use and the wicked sex life I was living. However, I had heard from God, and I would not stop holding on.

Cheriamor was still not eating right or dressing and looking like her daddy was making about a thousand dollars a week in the late eighties. Like I said, we usually didn't even have a television, and she didn't have many toys to play with. Mattie was doing a great job helping out with letting us come over and wash. She would send us home with food and would buy little things for ReRe. Most of what she had was from Mattie. We left most of her nice clothes and toys at Mattie's house in part because we spent so much time there. We didn't have much at our house.

Then it happened. I was pressing in harder to get closer to God and be a better parent those five and a half days a week. We would sing along with our cassette tapes on our way to church. While riding in the van, we would turn up the volume and sing along with gospel artists like Andre Crouch, the Mighty Clouds of Joy, and Al Green. We would be singing at the top of our voices. It felt so good there in the van—me and my baby singing about a new way, a new life, singing about God.

Things seemed to be changing when the devil stepped up his attack. The craving for the drugs and the sex got worse. Then it got worse. No, repeating myself was not a mistake. It got worse, or should I say it went to another level and continued climbing. It got worse and worse, third level. Then bottoming out started. I sold my van one night. It was a Saturday morning. I was walking to Mattie's house, thinking about how I was going to get to church on Sunday and work the following week, thirty miles away. When I got to Mattie's, I told her what had happened, and I told her I wanted to end it all, just take myself out, and she knew I meant it. Two things happened. First, she got on the phone with Reverend Leo Champion and told him about me. When I got on the phone, he made me promise to come to church the next day. Second, Mattie's actions stopped her from being an enabler.

I went to church the next day, and Reverend Champion's son, Reverend Gene Champion, spoke a word of healing into my life when he greeted me at the church door. As I walked up the front steps, here is what happened: Reverend Gene was around my age and had lived the same lifestyle as myself. His dad had told me this the day before as I spoke with him on the phone. Reverend Gene greeted me at the door and said, "Pastor told me all about it, but it's all over now. It's finished. You're all right now. Just go in there and get you some Jesus." Can I tell you all what I really was thinking on the inside? "Who in the h-e double hockey sticks is this clown talking to me about just going in and getting me some Jesus? It's over." But believe this if you will. As ReRe and I walked into that church, the peace of God that surpasses all understanding came over me. I really got into Sunday school, surprising myself, and afterward, the teacher asked if I was an elder. I told the class my story, and they just looked at me like, "Yeah, right." Well, this became our church home. That peace that came over me turned out to be my healing. For a while it really was finished that day. The pastor took me under his wing. I was instructed, constructed, and nurtured. I was put in classes to educate me and went out with teams to do street ministry. It was here at this church that I met and was educated by my new best friend, Reverend Pagel. I was living the life, a new life, a good life. The women of the church would take ReRe as soon as we got to church, redo her hair, love on her, and keep her in children's church. It was wonderful. We had a new extended family. We were so happy.

We came in the beginning of June, and by October, I preached my trial sermon and was licensed. We were finally living a good life again. I was being a really good parent again and loving it. My three kids and I did all kinds of things together. I felt like a family man. I was praying for a wife about twenty-three hours a day because I knew that the devil was going to come back stronger than ever before. I knew he could not come at me with something that was not a weakness. He only attacks in the areas you are weak in. I didn't want drugs. I wasn't even thinking about getting high. It was the last thing on my mind. I loved doing things for my kids and being a minister and even joined Reverend Pagel's ministry fellowship, Living Waters Ministry. He held classes on Monday evenings for ministers and elders, teaching them a deeper understanding of the scriptures. He taught us that as ministers and elders, it was important to not just know what the scriptures said but understand what they actually meant. There were about ten of us in his class. We would have class from 7:00 p.m. until 8:30 p.m. and then go out, have coffee, and talk about doing real ministry. We wanted to give, do, be there for, and meet people at the point of their needs. We all would bring our kids to everything and make them a part of the ministry. They sat in the classes and went with us when we went to preach.

One of us was always preaching somewhere. Sometime after we had been a part of this fellowship, ReRe wrote a church manual when she was about fifteen years old. In the manual, she talked about all the things we had talked about in these classes. She talked about what ministry was and was not. She talked about the role of every office and auxiliary within the church. She spent three years in these meetings from the age of five to eight. When I read the manual, it sounded just like a Living Waters Ministry handbook. Excuse me while I take a praise break. Glory! Hallelujah! Thank you, Jesus! Okay, I'm all right now. Let me sit back down, but I just had to get up and get my praise on for what God had done for my baby. I have to give God a praise whenever I think of His goodness and how He used this old ex-junkie to raise a daughter whose mind was shaped by the good that

God put around her and whose soul was not polluted by sin that tried to destroy me. Hallelujah.

Reverend Pagel was this awesome blind German preacher who only went to inner-city churches, mostly black churches. Reverend Champion allowed Reverend Pagel to travel as an evangelist to all different kinds of churches and denominations, where he would sing, play the organ, or preach, and sometimes, he would do all three on Sundays because he was in such high demand. Everybody wanted this white brother because he could sing and play like Ray Charles and sounded like a brother in the way he tuned up during his preaching. Everybody wanted Reverend Pagel. He was a great evangelist. He had an awesome style and could quote the entire Bible. Guess who became his assistant? Yep. You got it. Me and well, yeah, ReRe. The three of us were all over Milwaukee in black churches, white churches, big and small churches. I was an up-and-coming superstar preacher according to Reverend Pagel. He said I had great word illumination.

"Uh-oh! Houston is down. Satan caught him with a sucker punch, folks. Oh, what a shot. Houston is not moving yet. The count is at six, and he's trying to get up. Can he beat the count? Saved by the bell! His corner is trying everything they can to get him ready for the next round, but he's hurt!" I felt like the biggest trick ever known to mankind. You have to read Proverbs 7:1-27 to understand. Here's what happened. One night, my pastor, Reverend Champion, took me to a revival. He just wanted to spend some quality time somewhere with me. You have to understand that Reverend Champion was from the old school, unlike many pastors today where they just have you sit under them without developing hardly any relationship or having any real interaction. He, like Reverend Carpenter and Pastor Barclay, believed in raising a minister or an elder up in the ministry. We, in effect, became their sons in the Gospel, and with hands on-application, intervention, and interaction, they trained us. The church that we were at that evening was only a few blocks away from my house, so after church, he told me that he and the pastor had some business to work out on an upcoming revival. Seeing as how I was just a few blocks from home, he told me to go ahead, and the pastor would give him a ride home when they were done.

When I got in my car, the angel of darkness got in with me. The lie I told myself was I just wanted to drive through the "strip" to check out what was going on. The "strip" was an area on Twenty-eighth and North Avenue that was also called the scroll. This is where all the pimps, prostitutes, whores, hustlers, robbers, thieves, and thugs hung out, going in and out the bars. When I got there, I saw this gorgeous, totally well-groomed, big-legged, dark-skinned cutie pie. I pulled over, got her attention, and asked her into the car. I pulled around the corner to a dark street, and we hopped in the backseat, and I did my best interpretation of the "bunny rabbit special." Three and a half seconds later, we were pulling back onto the main street, and I let her out. I was not tempted to go with her to get high as she had asked. She tried everything she could to entice me to go with her (remember what I said earlier about the smoke houses and women). But all I wanted was what I got, and now I just wanted to get back home to my baby. The devil had my nose opened now, so the next night, this big ugly magnet drags me back to the same location, to the same spot, and I see this same gorgeous creature looking sexier than the night before. She hops into the car, and before I could say anything, she says, "Let's go to my girlfriend's house. She likes to get down too, and we can do this thing right." She got no objection from me. We walked into her girlfriend's apartment, and there stood probably one of the sexiest women I had ever seen. I spent money that night. They got high, and I got just what I wanted. When they ran out of drugs, I spent more money. They kept getting high, and I kept getting what I wanted.

As the night began to whine into morning and I let on that I was about to leave, the two of them talked privately just for a second. They understood that I didn't want any drugs, the smoke wasn't bothering me, and I was not tempted at all by them smoking, but I was now totally sexed out and they were about to lose their good "thang." I was, in fact, getting dressed to leave. Then it happened. That gorgeous dark-skinned cutie pie turned into the devil's princess. She pretended to give me a kiss and actually gave me a "shotgun blast." This is when one person will take a long hit on the pipe, hold the smoke in their mouth, and then blow it into the mouth of someone else. I had told them that I had been clean for a short while, and she knew exactly what this would do to me. When I realized what had happened, I immediately pulled away from her, and in that split second, I prayed, "Oh, Lord, please don't let me get high." When you hit the pipe, you don't actually feel the effects of the drugs until you blow the smoke out. I blew the smoke out and immediately reached for that damned pipe. That was about 5:00 a.m., and eight hundred dollars lighter and eight hours later, I finally made it home. It was Saturday morning. I don't know how to put into words the way I felt all week. I tried for two days to come up with words to explain how I felt for this book. God didn't even think about giving me words to explain that week because there were none.

I prayed all week that I would not use on Friday. All I could think about was how far my little family had come. ReRe was now in kindergarten. She had nice clothes, nice toys, and a television. We would sometimes take Reverend Pagel out to eat. He had become a true part of our family. Reverend Pagel said that he thought I could be pastoring my own church in maybe five years. I prayed, I fasted, I praised God, I made vows, and I even gave money to this lady and her baby in the store so she wouldn't have to put part of her groceries back. I changed a flat tire in the rain for an ex-girlfriend. I was like a little kid trying to be good around their mama after doing something really bad at school, hoping to get a good report from her since getting home from school so my daddy wouldn't kill my bad little butt. But that didn't work with God. God would have none of it. None! God was tired of my little hardheaded butt. He whipped my butt and then put me on a punishment that lasted three years (Psalms 50:22-23). God didn't speak to me for a week, and when He did, if I asked about getting off drugs, he would just walk away. God would deal with me about anything but getting off drugs. I felt so bad, I wanted to quit the ministry, but Reverend Pegal said absolutely not. He said if I thought he was going to let me quit, I should come over to his house and he would turn off the light, then it would be a fair fight. One would think that a person like him (he was still a virgin at thirty-nine) would not want a backslidden minister who was now back on drugs being his assistant and driving him all around town.

He told me something that changed so much of how I looked at myself. It helped me through the next three years. He told me that God spoke to him that I was going to be the pastor and director of a ministry dealing with others just like myself one day. He told me other things that would happen in my life that I have gone on to do. He said that I would inspire thousands who were just like me. Things that pastors see in me now and things that I'm now living, Reverend Pagel saw and told me back in 1990. He didn't kick me to the curb. He carried me. He believed God said it, and he put his money where his mouth was. Being a big man, old Rev loved to eat. He told me I was going to still be his assistant, me and ReRe. With Reverend Pagel being blind, I learned how to lead him by using my arm. ReRe carried his Bible and opened the doors sometimes. Thus, in those three years with us being his assistants and him loving to eat every time we went somewhere, he paid for all three of us to eat. He did this for all three years in addition to putting gas in my car. There were times when he knew we didn't have any food at home, so he would take us grocery shopping and pay for it.

The next three years were worse than words can tell. By then, I was done. I was a dead man walking (Ezekiel 37:1-11). Maybe someone else would not have cared about how they were living as long as they got to be the assistant to the evangelist and sit in the pulpit every Sunday, but not me. You have to understand that for me, I felt like dung, like crap. I felt such condemnation every Sunday morning, and not just then but all week long. All I wanted was to be a real man of God. I wanted this more than life itself. My cousin and former pastor had shared so many stories with me about his father and about our grandfather who were both presiding elders in the church. He shared how they were such awesome preachers and pastors and so well respected in Georgia. I now just wanted to be like my roots. I had experienced a taste of honey, and that's worse than none at all. I had to get back to where I was before the fall. By now, Reverend Pagel and I and—you got it—ReRe, were at church two times a week and twice on some Sundays. Reverend Pagel and I spent hours on the phone reading, talking, and praying. We went to revivals together. He shared my struggles with the other members of the fellowship. No one made it easy for me, but no one condemned or put me down or tried to put me out. Everyone felt the same about my calling as Reverend Pagel did, including pastors and elders we met at the churches he spoke at. The only thing I lied to Reverend Pagel about was having sex. I knew he knew though. Have you ever been scared every minute of the day? I was scared, never knowing when someone at church would say, "I saw Reverend Houston coming out the dope house today." I held my breath all the time.

Poor ReRe, she was back to the half-filled kitchen cabinets, no television, and clothes that didn't fit. Yes, back to Mattie's house. I was afraid I would lose ReRe to the state. She was in school now, and every Friday I was late. I would be high when I got there to pick her up. For sure, I was far worse than I had been before, and I was running out of time before she would really know and understand what I was doing and how she was living. Between the fear of being found out at church, losing the total respect of Reverend Pagel, losing ReRe, and my business, I was about to lose my mind. Something had to change.

I did well in running my business, parenting, and functioning as a minister from Sunday morning until Friday at 3:00 p.m. I prayed all week, believing this weekend would be different. I always told the members of the fellowship ministry, "Not this weekend." And they knew I meant it, but every weekend, I fell. Every Sunday I started over again. I lived in hell for the whole three years. Things kept getting worse and worse. I could not hide any longer. Then one day, Neoccesha and Nicky told me they heard that I was a junkie. I could not lie. Gone were the Volvo, the Lincoln Town Car, the Cadillac, my Fiat Spider, my five-thousand-dollar watch, three-thousand-dollar ring, and five-hundred-dollar gold chain. I stood there and looked them right in the face and said, "Yes, it's true. It's been a few years now, and I'm almost out." I spoke with confidence like the old pro liar I was. I learned through my many years in the street you always have to stand strong. Besides, I was Daddy, and I had to be strong for my kids. They had a world of respect for me. They were in high school now, not little kids any more. I had to be cool and calm. I had to keep parenting, keep being Daddy. At this point I only had a few changes of clothes, but I kept myself clean and always talked to them about having to keep up their grades and get ready for college. I wouldn't let Neoccesha hang with certain girls or talk with certain types of boys. I gave Neoccesha driving lessons myself. Nicky was three years younger, but he and I would hang out a lot together. To this day, I have not told a joke they didn't laugh at. I kept them talking, listening, and laughing. I made sure they saw me with blueprints every week. I made sure they saw me as a working man, as a businessman, and always in church.

However, my world was falling down. Most people knew by now that I was using again. Reverend Pagel and I had both left Reverend Champion's church, and I was at my family's church, where all my family and half the church knew what I had been through in recent years. But my lie was that I no longer used. So I had to go across town to use in order to keep up the front. I think people at least wanted to believe me because I was an outstanding single parent with ReRe. I was always at her school during the week. I had quit my company for a while and got on welfare so I could be a stay-at-home dad for her. I didn't allow ReRe to watch certain programs like *The Simpsons* with obnoxious characters such as Bart Simpson or shows like *Married With Children*. ReRe knew if she was caught watching these programs or others like them, we would fight. She knew if she was somewhere and someone else was watching these shows, she had to go to another room. I went so far as to tell her teachers that she could not participate in Halloween activities because we were saved. I believe the stance I took as a parent helped to make her the person she is today. I walked her to school at first, then when she got older, I walked her to the corner by the school. Then two blocks from school. Then three blocks from school. Finally, I just walked her to the corner by our house. I cried the first time she told me I didn't have to walk her to the corner because she and her friends were going to walk together. I sat there thinking how far she and I had come. She was so happy. She had no idea we were about to be put out.

Things got worse. Neoccesha called and told me her mother could not keep her and Nicky in private school any longer because I had not been paying my part. She was in twelfth grade now and had been in private school since the second grade. When she said she wouldn't graduate with her class and with her friends all because of my addiction, something died inside of me. This was my firstborn, my Peanut as we called her. We had been so close. I remembered when Neoccesha, Nicky, their mom, and I were supposed to go to Great America. Neoccesha was about eight years old at that time. I told her mother that I wanted to stay home and just do nothing because I had worked hard that week. I gave her mom the keys to the van and some money. I remember Peanut jumping out of the van telling her mother she wanted to stay home with her daddy. We just went in the house and took a nap. She was so happy that day just being with me.

Even though I gave Neoccesha and Nicky money when I had it and I tried to see them when I wasn't totally strung out, I am so regretful that I was able to maintain the relationship that we had when they were young before I was strung out on the pipe. I regret not being there for them and raising them like the father that they needed and deserved and like the father I truly wanted to be. When their mother and I broke up, I regret not maintaining a stronger presence in their life regardless of the relationship between her and me. Neoccesha and Nicky are really wonderful kids who turned out great in spite of all that they went through.

Things progressively got worse for me. I was now spending twelve hundred dollars a week. The worse things got, the harder I pressed in as a parent. I finally got Neoccesha's love back although she was still hurt and angry. I kept loving my kids. I kept trying to parent. She and Nicky saw me going to church every Sunday, working like a dog during the week, and taking care of Cheriamor. I was trying to do the best I could. I would give them money when I had it and buy them things when I could. It wasn't as though I didn't do anything for them; I just didn't do as much as I should have the way I should have. Mattie would buy them clothes for Easter, Mother's Day, Father's Day, and Christmas. She would also buy them clothes for school and give them to me to give to them. She no longer would give me any money. Not a penny.

The further I fell into the abyss of drugs, the more I tried to step up my game as parent. Nicky and I talked like two old men. Although I was Daddy, I made sure I gave Nicky that friendship and time a son needed to feel loved by his dad, or so I thought. My son manned up and allowed me to spoil the girls. He would let me know he had my back and that he knew I had his. I had his love, but he never really told me how hurt he was for me not really giving him what he needed. I never found out until writing this book just how hurt he was when I had neglected spoiling him along with the girls. Thank you for being my little twelve-year-old man not wanting to hurt your dad. What an awesome son you've always been. I love you, son. I had done very well with Nicky and Neoccesha when they were growing up until I got on that pipe. I had to do the same for ReRe even though I was on drugs. As I said before, I was determined to give her a mother's love.

I raised ReRe just like a mother would do. I taught her how to pray, how to go potty, how to sit like a little lady. She started carrying a purse everywhere she went when she was six years old and has never stopped. We did her homework together. We talked about everything together. I learned how to be a broke junkie daddy and take two or three dollars and take my daughter to Lincoln Park and buy my baby an ice cream cone. I taught her how to swing. We would go for thirty-minute rides when there was gas, and I would take her to visit people so she wouldn't be isolated. When we were on welfare, we didn't have a car, so we walked all over town or took the buses wherever we had to go. We never missed one church service.

As a minister, I had keys to the church; and even when we had to take the bus, we were the first to get there. I was responsible for opening up the church. I had one suit and one sports jacket. ReRe had three dresses. I remember once when we didn't have a car and had left church one Sunday. It was cold and snowy out. We were on the corner at the bus stop, which was right by the church. One of the deacons drove up in his big pretty car, waved, turned, and went in the same direction we were going. He didn't even think to offer us a ride. It was okay. I had done this to myself, so a lot of people didn't trust me, but what about my baby? I began to chase her around the mailbox until the bus came. This kept us warm. No matter what, I was determined to keep parenting although things kept getting worse. Parenting was my sanity.

Then we finally lost our apartment again. Now here we were, back in the hood. Back again where it all started. I was so bad off and hurting at this point. It was like pain was in every part of my life. I no longer knew life without pain. I cried, and I mean I cried hard every day. And yes, I prayed, and I went to the revivals. Reverend Pagel and I continued to pray together. I was still his assistant, but things had gone from bad to worse. Then something happened that really shook me up and was a part of my turning around. Reverend Pagel and I were at church. This prophet had come in from out of town for a revival. After he had preached, he did a prayer line and began to go down the aisle, laying hands and praying for people. He would tell people things about who they were. Things that we knew to be true about the individual and some things we didn't know. It was for sure this man was a real prophet. All of us ministers and elders were at the end of the line, and when he got to me, he just stopped and looked at me and he said, "You're supposed to be doing just what I'm doing." And he went on to say some things that Reverend Pagel and other pastors had been telling me for the past six years about God's hands on me to use me in ministry. As a matter of fact, he told me to get out of the line, and he continued to pray for others who were in line behind me. After this, things, yet again, got worse for a little while.

Finally, I went to God screaming and hollering like a crazy madman. I was just about a half of an inch from shaking my finger in God's face. I had just spent four thousand dollars on a five-day binge. I had about five hours of sleep in those five days and maybe had eaten a few snacks along the way but no meals. That was it. Like the prodigal son in Luke 15:11-24, I finally came to myself. I was driving my car, and I almost tore the steering wheel off the column as I screamed out and asked God, "Why won't you heal me?" Then I told God that if I had to live as a junkie, I didn't want to live at all. I began to vow my way out, telling God that if He would set me free, I would never do drugs again in my life. This was an unconditional surrender because I said "no matter what." And my promise to God was that I would go back like Harriet Tubman as a thief in the night and get the others and bring them to the lighthouse. The next day, I went and took my physical to get into a one-year Christian-ministry rehab, and I never looked back.

I have always been a mama's baby. I don't think any mama could love her child any more than my mama loved me. When I was a kid, my friends would tease me about how my mama showed me so much love. My family talked about how she loved me. They would say, "You know if anything happened to you, Aunt Tab [that's what they called my mama] would die." We were so close. I could talk with her about anything I was dealing with. We were not just mother and son, but we were friends. We always talked more than anyone ever would believe. She always told me to believe in God and trust Him no matter what, and it paid off that day in 1993 when God turned my life around. She was thirty-seven when she had me, and although she only went to the sixth grade, she was a very wise lady. She was the matriarch of the family in Milwaukee after her sister died in 1960. A lot of times, she could be a pain in the butt because she was such a big baby, but she was a lover. She loved her nephews, her nieces, and her grandchildren with such great compassion. She always told me to stay alive and not to go to jail because she would die if something happened to me, and I knew she meant it. God kept me through a few gun battles and many more dangerous ordeals for my mama's sake. I remember getting hit in the family car. The car was totaled, but I walked away. People at the scene could only look in disbelief when I climbed out from where the door used to be. I learned a lot about being a parent from God using the lessons my mother taught me by showing me a real mother's love. I always tried to give my kids what my mother gave me. I didn't realize I was trying to be my mother, only in a manly type of way.

While working on this book and talking with ReRe, she told me that she never missed having a mother. She said she never felt a void in her childhood growing up. She went on to say that she never felt anything but loved as a child. She was happy and felt that she had a normal childhood. When she was older, every Mother's Day, she always bought me a card. She was eight years old when I went away to get help, and at eight, she never had any idea that I was on drugs or that we were poor. When she didn't have a TV, she didn't miss a beat. She would just play school, house, or church. She never cared much for dolls. When she played house, she was always a little "Aunt Tab," always telling the younger women in the family how to handle their kids. In school, she was the teacher, and in church she played every role. As a freshman in high school, Cheriamor, of her own accord, made a vow of chastity by joining Demoiselle 2 Femme.

Today, Cheriamor, at twenty-five years of age, has a bachelor's degree in fashion design and has a license to sell real estate. To her, selling homes is about more than just the sell. She has a ministry heart and always wants to help people get the home that is just right for them. She works for a Christian health-care business. She is filled with the Holy Ghost, always active in doing ministry in the church, and saving herself in purity until she meets her husband. Her heart's desire is to become a fashion designer, to have her own business, as well as to minister to youth and young adults. God gave me a miracle in my daughter. This little baby that I took when she was one year old, this little baby that I had learned to parent, has grown into such an awesome young lady that I am so proud of. She was part of my inspiration and determination to get off drugs and to never allow the devastation of drugs and the drug lifestyle to touch her. My other two children, Neoccesha and Nicky, were the other part of my inspiration because I desperately desired to renew and restore my relationship with my children.

There are several reasons I wrote this book, one being I want to tell people who are going through drug addiction that not only is there life after drugs, but also that you don't have to stop living because you are on drugs. No matter what you may be going through, just know that God will see you through. If you hold on and do your part, God will do His part. I don't care how impossible it may seem to hold on; don't sink into the abyss. Look at your kids, look at your parents, look at your spouse, and get strength and determination to hold on and come out. I don't care how tired you get; just don't quit, hold on. I don't care how things keep getting worse; still hold on. I don't care how much you have to cry sometimes. Just hold on. I don't care how many people talk about you or how crazy you have acted; just hold on. If you will love and trust God, if you can only believe, praise Him even when you are still out there, for the Bible says, "Let everything that has breath praise the Lord." This means even the junkie, the alcoholic, and the prostitute can praise Him because you're still alive. You are not a hypocrite because at this stage you're not professing but praising. Yes, St. John 14:21 lets me know I couldn't love Him right until I could obey Him, so I believed in Him to change my heart so I could obey and love Him right. He will fix it. He did it for me, and I know He will do it for you. Hold on to those kids. Don't let the state get your kids. Love them now, and they will love you later. They are your blessing from the kingdom of God (Luke 18:15-16). Stay in church, you and your kids, no matter how you have to dress, no matter what you've done the week before or the night before. Show God how bad you want it, and your change will come. Psalms 37:22-24 says the following:

For those blessed by Him shall inherit the earth,
But those cursed by Him shall be cut off.

The steps of a good man are ordered by the LORD,
And He delights in his way.

Though he fall, he shall not be utterly cast down;
For the LORD *upholds him with His hand*

Remember, man looks on the outward appearance, but God looks at the heart. If He sees you with all sincerity trying to climb out the hole, He will help you.

I also wrote this book because I want you to know that there is life after drugs. I don't care what you have been through; somebody has been through more, came out, and gone on to do great things. I have been clean since September 27, 1993, and the Lord has blessed this ex-junkie to do things I never dreamed of while I was on drugs. Besides the blessing of my daughter coming through our life together, untouched by drugs or the stink of sin life, I have ministered to many on the streets whose lives were messed up by addiction and saw God change their lives, including one well-known NFL player who has gone on to remain clean since 1996. I have spent my own money and sent men and women away to a Christian ministry. I have ministered at rehabilitation centers and jails, and now I am a director and pastor, along with my wife, of a small drug ministry providing housing and rehabilitation for others as God provided for me through a Christian ministry.

But get this—God is funny in the way that He will bless you sometimes not only spiritually but naturally as well. Through the General Services Administration (federal government) and a general contractor, I got a job as a subcontractor, and little old me, the ex-junkie from Milwaukee, was blessed to paint then incoming Senator Barack Obama's office suite in Chicago. Yes, that's right—me. I got to paint the office of the future president of the United States when he became Senator of Illinois. This was no coincidence, no happenstance, but this had God's DNA all over it. God saw me in my future even when I was on drugs. Also, after 9/11, during a time when contractors were being scrutinized, for four months

I worked painting the FBI office in Chicago. But funniest of all was me, of all people, Pookie, the ex-junkie, the ex-player, for about three months, painted the Drug Enforcement Agency offices. That's funny, God. Me, one of the biggest ex-junkies got to paint the DEA. I know God is good and He is faithful and He will restore many of the years that sin has taken away.

I am shouting all these blessings from the rooftop because I want all my brothers and sisters still going through the struggle to know that I am working on another contract for the glory of God. A healing and deliverance contract, a contract to let you know this: Don't stop living. There is life after drugs. However, I can't emphasize this next point enough. When you get out, you can't just pick a church and say "I'm going there." You must be lead by the Spirit of God to go to the right church meant for you. So many people have been hurt or discouraged by ending up in the wrong place. Every church, yes, even those professing the name of Jesus, will not accept us in their churches. We will never fit in or be one of them because of the lifestyle we've come out of. You must find a church that operates in the power of God, that preaches and lives holiness, a church that shows the love of God and has no respect of person. A church that is about ministry and sees everyone through the eyes of Christ. Every church does not meet this criteria, but there are some that are out there.

I wrote this book for you, my brother and my sister, because I know how we are when we are on drugs. I am still just a brother off the corner. I have not forgotten where I came from. I still feel your pain, my brother and my sister, black or white, young or old. I will always be one of you. I can never forget the nightmare of twenty-seven years of drug addiction and the life from hell that went with it. It's like being a veteran. I've gone through the war against the drug life and fought the battle of life and death on the street, lived to tell about it and to bring someone else out. Yes, as long as my folks are out there, I will be somewhere out there still in the struggle to bring someone out. I'll never go in the closet about where I've been. I know us. We love it when one of us makes it out and comes back in a real way to help a brother out in love.

Now at this point, I might just be talking to people that have been there, 'cause a lot of people will take this out of context and think I am bragging; not so. I don't mind saying that as I sit here in our four-bedroom house with my wife of over two years and a nice van in the driveway and a CTS in the garage, I have tears running down my face. There may be many who don't believe that what has happened for me could happen for them.

I used to sit and think how and when or if ever I would live in a nice house again, have a nice car again, and Lord knows I never believed a woman of God would ever have anything to do with a man of my background.

I know with God all things are possible, but I just didn't think it would happen for me. You see, about my old life, the half has not been told. So when I look at how and where I live, who I'm married to, I want to tell all my hurting brothers and sisters, we can live again or live for the very first time. See, I know that many may not show signs on the outside of wanting to be free 'cause that "thang" of drug addiction is insane, and people that haven't been there won't understand that on the inside, most of us really want to be free, rid of this monkey on our back. We are hurting for our parents, our kids, our spouses, and we really want to live again even though it might not show. But that "thang" is insane. We want our lives back. We just want to be free, but that "thang" is insane. It is the very definition of insanity. There is a difference between the ones that don't care and the ones that do. They may both look the same but they are not. The ones that do care, they might keep going back, but on the inside, they are clawing to get out. Remember, things are not what they always look like on the outside. People tried to tell me I really didn't care and that I really didn't want it, but I knew different. I just couldn't walk away until God healed me. Every day, I think about how I suffered and the ones that didn't make it. Every day, I deal with someone that has a loved one still out there, and they are dying because their loved one is dying. Every day, I think about my mother and how she would have felt if she had not died before I went all the way out there. Lord Jesus, thank you.

Although we only have one ministry house opened at this time, we continue to believe God for more ministry houses established in more cities, ministry houses for men and women that want to change. Ministry houses that will help tear down as much of the devil's kingdom as possible. I actually believe God that I will receive enough proceeds from this book to establish these houses. I know I can't help everybody, but I'll help all that I can.

I'm reminded of a story that went like this: there was a man walking along the seashore, and there had been a great storm the night before. The storm had washed thousands of fish ashore. As he walked, he was picking up fish, throwing them back in the water. Someone approached him and asked him what he was doing, and he replied, "I'm trying to save the fish." The other person said, "You can't possibly make a difference because there are so many fish washed ashore." The man that was throwing the fish in the water reached down, picked up another fish, threw it in the water, and said, "I made a difference to that one." All I am is a nobody trying to make a difference in somebody's life.

Last but not least, I also wrote this book for all the children and young people who have parents that are living this dysfunctional lifestyle, to encourage you that you can come out of this dysfunction and achieve great things. You can be the sanity, the light that will eventually heal your family and make them whole. One of the greatest things that I've experienced as a man, next to God's deliverance, was while writing this book, my youngest daughter told me that while growing up, she never realized the hardship of how she was growing up. She never felt neglected or ever missed having a mother's love because I met all her needs, and she never realized that she should have had two parents. Even to this moment, when I think about what she said, it brings tears to my eyes that God would use me, in all my dysfunction, to raise such a wonderful daughter. To this day, as I stated before, every Mother's Day, my daughter sends me a Mother's Day card. Cheriamor is a testimony of strength within herself. As she got older, I shared my past lifestyle with her—those things that she might not have understood as a child. She latched onto the good part that she saw in me and the love that she felt from me. One day, she will tell her own story, and what an awesome story that will be. To all those kids who may have parents that are still struggling in this area, you must realize that the adversities of your parents can drive you to be an awesome success story because your adversities can be your stepping stone to success instead of your excuse for failure. Perhaps someone else is raising you right now because your parents aren't around because of drugs. Don't get bitter; get better. Use your experience to be the person that you dream of on the inside. If Cheriamor could do it, so can you. God doesn't love her any more than He loves you. I left to go get help when she was eight years young. I had to tell her the truth about why I was leaving. She had to stay with her auntie for a while, but yet, she still came through strong and successful. So can you.

After a couple of years, I got my daughter back from her auntie and finished raising her, putting her through high school and college. Parents that are still out there, let me again remind you: please don't forget your children. Don't let the pipe, the alcohol, or the lifestyle take them away from you. Love them even through your dysfunction. Let them be your inspiration to get out. With God and time, He can heal and restore your family. I had asked my children to share with me some of their thoughts about life with me when I was out there on drugs that would express how they felt growing up. ReRe told me she could think of nothing better than a letter she framed and sent me in 1999 for Father's Day. It went like this:

Dear Daddy,

Though we have been apart over the years, your love is still close to my heart, and I still feel as if you were near. No matter what people say, there has never been a day in my life that I have ever wished I had a better father. You may not have been able to give me the best but I am thankful for what you have struggled to get me for 8 years of my life. For all that you have given to me my love will never change. I thank God for blessing me to have the best dad in the world. When I look back I smile for all the good times we shared. I thank God for the bad things that didn't get worse, and I look forward to the future. Happy Father's Day! Thank you for being the best father you could.

Your daughter,
Cheriamor

My son, Nicky, sent the following:

So Proud of You

Although, I've always loved my dad when I was a young boy, around five or six years old he seemed to have had more patience with my older sister, Neocchesa and was more quick tempered and stern with me. Later my dad seemed to be more of the big brother type with me but more of the father figure with Neoccesha although I knew he did love me as a son.

I believed that what actually happened was because my dad had missed out on having that fun loving big brother, pal type of fatherly relationship with his dad who was older when he came along and a southerner from the old school. That he gave me what he had missed instead of giving me what I was missing which was that nurturing type of fatherly relationship that he and his dad had. I loved that cool part of my dad that he showed me of himself but I longed for and missed the father figure. He has always been able to make me laugh regardless of the times or situations. He has always given me good instructions as a young adult and as I became a young man he gave me understanding in how to carry myself in business pursuits. But I've always missed that father son relationship because too often he was my pal and big brother instead of my father.

I was twelve when my dad got strung out on the pipe. I didn't get to see him as often during his addiction because my sister and I had moved with my mom to another neighbor in Milwaukee. So actually what I got was less of what I had been getting but I never complained because my dad was so confident that he was being a super dad and regardless of how bad I was hurting I just had to much love in my heart to shoot him down. I guess there was to much serenity in seeing him in all his pride and glory because I never seen my dad depressed. Perhaps because my dad is such a great story teller and stand up comic I had to accept the relationship we had rather than lose this fun loving pal. Although, I was hurt because of the lack of closeness and togetherness that I needed in a father-son relationship at that time I always knew my dad's faith would one day bring him through. His faith and determination to be somebody in my eyes would materialize. So, although he didn't become what I needed in life until later I'm thankful to God that he made it. Today I am relieved and happy to be able to say to anyone that he through God fought the devil a very long and difficult battle and although he came through with many scars, he made it, and now I am very blessed to have both the big brother pal and nurturing father relationship with my dad. Dad I'm so proud of you for having turned your life around. People may be able to say something about your past but I can say "how you like him now."

Love ya,
Nicky Mudd

And finally, my oldest daughter, Neoccesha, sent me this perspective, which I would like to use to end this chapter with. I think she says it best. Thank you, Neoccesha, Nicky, and Cheriamor. You all are the loves of my life.

Obedience is better than sacrifice...

One day a mother told her three year old daughter to put on her new shoes so that they could go to Wal-Mart. The child refused to put the shoes on and left them in the middle of the floor. When her mother asked her to pick the shoes up and put them on, the child quickly ran to her room and came back with her favorite teddy bear. The child gently put the teddy bear in the mother's arms and gave her mother a hug and a kiss but still refused to put on the shoes. The mother smiles and grabs her Wal-Mart bag and the receipt for the items in the bag and they head out to Wal-Mart. When the mother and child arrived at Wal-Mart the child sees the new Barney toy that she has been wanting for months. The mother tells the child no, not until she puts on her new shoes. The child began to cry and make such a fuss that the mother picks up the child and leaves the store immediately. The child, seeing that her mother cut the shopping trip short instead of giving in to her tears, tries another approach. When the child got home she gave the mother another one of her prized stuffed animal and tons of hugs and kisses.

Next week the same thing happened. The mother told the child to put on her new shoes so they could go to Wal-Mart. The child refused to put on the new shoes and like last week she gave her mother another one of her prized stuffed animals and tons of hugs and kisses. Again the mother smiles and grabs her Wal-Mart bag and they head out to Wal-Mart to do some shopping. The child again sees Barney and begs her mother for the stuffed animal but again the mother says "No, not until you put on your new shoes." Again the child begins to cry and the shopping trip is cut short. The mother and child continue this cycle for another couple of weeks.

The next month the mother tells the child to get dressed

so that they could go to Wal-Mart. The child runs to her room and puts on her new shoes to go to Wal-Mart. When the mother and child arrive Barney is all sold out. The child begins to cry and asks her mom "why did you wait so long to buy Barney?" The mother then asked the child "Why did you wait so long to wear your new shoes?" The mother then let the child in on her surprise, she told her daughter that she had bought the Barney months ago and pulled Barney out of the Wal-Mart bag she always brought with her. She told her daughter that the only reason why they were at Wal-Mart was so the little girl can take a picture with her new Barney and her new shoes which matched Barney's shoes.

- The child represents us as Christians
- The shoes are the task God asks us to do
- The teddy bears are our sacrifices (attempts to compromise with God)
- The hugs and kisses are our prayers and time spent with God
- The mother or parent Represents God
- The Wal-Mart bag represents God's Plan for our life

Just like this child we try to give sacrifices to God because we don't like the task God is asking us to do or the people or things God is asking us to give up. We spend hours in prayer, reading the Word of God, but refuse to be obedient to his request.*

My father was good at sacrificing. He sacrificed money; I would get $20 just for washing my grandmother's dishes. He sacrificed quality time when he was able. I remember one time he told me, my brother, and my cousin to hop in the car he was taking us to get a soda. He drove us from Milwaukee to the Green Bay Packer stadium in Green Bay where we got a soda. My father laughed and talked to us all the way there and back, not many adults spent that type of quality time.

Then one day my father put me and my brother down and picked up the pipe. My world changed, I became bitter and rebellious because I lost hope. My father kept up religious appearances, he prayed, went to bible study, and studied under great ministers in the pulpit but I was not buying it. I would not allow him to reconcile our once loving relationship; I made every effort to remind him of how much I did not respect him. My younger brother and sister kept their opinions to themselves and attempted to forgive and respected him as our father. I, the first born, and a daddy's girl, FLAT OUT REFUSED to respect or forgive him. Although he earnestly tried to be a father to me, I made it my business to make his life miserable and had the nerve to try to justify it. Then one day he decided to be obedient to what God was asking him to do. He submitted his will over to God and went to a Christian rehabilitation ministry to get his life back together. A few years later after he had gotten cleaned up God **began** to reconcile our relationship.

My father's life is like the little girl with the new shoes. She was cheating herself out of something that was already hers and so was my dad. Just like the mother had already purchased the Barney for her daughter, God had already reconciled the relationship with my father and his children. The little girl in the story was not allowed to receive her Barney until she was obedient to her mother, just like my father was not allowed to receive the reconciliation with his children until he was obedient to God.

The reason why I picked the topic of obedience rather than sacrifice for my father's book is because I have a message to all of you parents that are out there struggling with your drug addiction. If your relationship with your child/ren has been severed **DO NOT GIVE UP NO MATTER HOW BAD IT SEEMS!** Me and My father's relationship was really bad, no one really wanted to be in the same room with us once we got started, mainly due to me picking for a confrontation. Being a child of a drug addict caused me to become angry, bitter, rebellious, disrespectful, self destructive and above all else unforgiving to anyone who betrayed my trust. As a teenager and young adult I had no respect for a parent on drugs I felt that it was selfish, a sign of weakness, and a copout of being a parent. In the end I realize that the same person I saw as selfish, weak, and failing to be a parent was the one who took the ultimate steps to restore our relationship. My father's courage to step out of his comfort zone and face the hard cold reality was the deciding factor in our relationship. His obedience to God brought forth restoration and healing from God. There is no greater love than the love a parent has for their child. As a parent you can bring forth that restoration and healing to your family through obedience to God. No Matter how bad it seems God **can and will** restore. Today I love and respect my father more than I did yesterday because of his obedience to God and the restoration and healing that it brought to our family.

With sincerity, respect, and encouragement,

The proud daughter of Raymond

* The original source of this story is unknown.

My oldest daughter, Neoccesha

My only son, Nicky

My baby daughter, Cheriamor

Neoccesha, ReRe, and Ray

Pastor Ray and Pastor Colleen

Chapter Two

Altering of the Mind

Romans 13:11-14, Ephesians 5:18

The first thing a person should understand about drugs is that it alters the mind and the natural body chemistry. The body has a natural chemistry that is a person's "normal self." It is this state that the person is in before they've ever used drugs. It is this state that tells us to eat when we are hungry, to go to bed when we are tired, or to run when we sense danger. Then when you put a foreign chemical, a foreign substance in your body long enough and consistent enough, the normal chemistry that defines you will change. Now you no longer feel normal unless you have a cigarette, a drink, or some drug. You must now continue to have whatever will get you to that feeling of what has been created as your new norm.

Man has a certain expectation for feeling normal. He desires it. He longs for it. Thus, his new chemical makeup makes him believe that all he or she needs is that next drug, that next drink, that next fix, that next hit, that next snort to make them feel normal. But it all will fail because sooner or later, the drug, the foreign substance, is going to take over. Some people have more of an addictive nature, and they fall sooner, but everyone will eventually fall if they continue putting foreign substances in their body. They will be entrapped by that substance.

In some cases, such as with cocaine, this is taken a step further. With drinking or cigarettes, a person may have a strong desire for what they need, but with cocaine, that part of the brain that controls all our desires is actually altered by the cocaine use. Yes, cocaine actually alters the brain waves that control our desires. The brain is actually trained to desire drugs. Now what you have is a new functioning brain wave pattern trained like a circus monkey to desire and crave cocaine. Your desire has turned to control.

It is therefore important to understand that when you are doing drug ministry or talking with a loved one about their addiction, you must approach them with knowledge. If you do not understand that they are now functioning from their new norm trained by and held captive by drug dependency, you will only be frustrated in your attempts to help them, and your ministry that was meant to help will only fail. You must understand that their new nature is what causes them to go out and spend the rent money, the food money, the children's money. We cannot understand this abnormal behavior. It is not rational to us, but it is their norm because drugs have trained their brain to think and act differently.

I loved smoking weed with a passion for twenty years almost every day. I snorted cocaine from around 1973 until 1985 off and on. It was cool; I could take it or leave it. Drinking was really to make me feel cool and give me courage to talk to women. But after I got high from smoking cocaine the first time, I cannot tell you how good it was. There are no words known to mankind that I could use. I can tell you this as an understatement: cocaine had sex beat hands down! If you think this is appealing, you are a damned fool. Run! No, the opposite way. Away from. While in the beginning of this outrageous high, I didn't even care about being hooked for the first year. I knew it was wrong, but I didn't want to stop. My norm was altered. This was the new me. With this in mind, perhaps those of you who have never been on cocaine can get some idea of the junkies' abnormal behavior and way of thinking.

Some substances we desire, and some substances control us. A strong desire can really be hard to deal with, but how do you handle something that is actually controlling you? How do you handle something that has total control over your life? This is a true form of slavery. If you are going to effectively minister to those in this predicament, you must not take personal the things that they do (although this may be hard if the person is a loved one) because they are reacting from an altered brain chemistry. This altered state is demanding to be fed just like the normal hungry person would do, only their abnormal self is crying for drugs and not food.

Oftentimes, the person that is trying to help the addict runs into problems and frustration because they feel that just by talking logistics or quoting scriptures, the person should reason within themselves and come back to reality and turn their life around. This is not likely to happen. Working with individuals with substance-abuse issues is a "calling." The person in this ministry or venue must have understanding, patience, wisdom, and the power of the Holy Ghost. They must think and see things as the addict sees them in order to bring them out. I have had success in ministering to these individuals because basically, I am just "one of the fellows." I have walked where they have walked and felt what they feel. I have lied to and conned myself and others, so I know where they are and where they are coming from. You must prepare yourself to see things from their perspective. It's an added plus.

There is another problem that we have in dealing with those addicted to drugs and alcohol. Many times, we have raised our children with the correct morals and values. We have raised them to never do drugs or drink excessively, but somehow they go out and get addicted anyway. We still want to see them as good children doing bad things, but we must realize that this is not the child that we raised. This is not the good kid doing the bad thing, but somewhere along the line, our child has graduated, and now they are bad kids doing bad things.

The biggest mistake my parents made was that they loved me so much that they trusted my word without proof or holding me accountable while I was growing up. I was not who I claimed to be. I played it by ear and told them what they wanted to hear. It does not matter about all the baby pictures you look at of "little Susie" or "little Johnnie." You must realize that the drug addict standing before you is a completely different person, and the drugs that they crave has turned them from that "good kid" to another junkie that lives to get that next high and will do whatever it takes to get it. Even if they are not the "stickup" man holding the gun, they have gone bad. It does not matter if your child is using or selling. They've gone bad. It does not matter if your child is pimping or being pimped. They have gone bad. Both individuals are stepping in the same mess of drug dependency, the same mess of sin. So just because your baby was raised right at the point of addiction, they are no better than the kid that was raised wrong. The only differences that you have between the two is that there was a foundation that was instilled in the one that through prayer and much work can pull them back sooner while the other will still need a foundation built, which can take much longer.

When I was hooked, I always knew that when I got ready to stop, all I had to do was come back to God. I knew the road wouldn't be easy, but God could and would heal me. Little did I know that because I had turned my back on God, the chastisement would be so very hard. I thank God I didn't get what I had coming (death), but I got the twins, grace and mercy. God knew how to deal with me, and He did. He allowed things to become hard because I never cared about things that came easy. Now, I would not go back to drugs even at gunpoint. I had taken God for granted once, and I won't do it again.

I have a serious abrasion with most thirty-day programs, and the continual vicious cycle of addicts returning to these programs explains why. I feel it takes a period of ninety days to develop a new habit, and it also takes ninety days for the body to be cleansed from the poison chemical and dependencies of that habit. Others will say that this will only take thirty days. It could happen, but for most, it doesn't. At the time I went away to get help, God let me know that He had healed me spiritually, but I needed to be healed in my mind and in body. I felt okay at thirty days, nice at ninety days, but healed at 365 days.

For the most part, I oppose secular programs that just "program" the addict with usual textbook jargon that provides no real inner healing. I believe that in order for the deliverance to be complete, the addict must be healed both naturally and spiritually. While I condemn no program that helps, because some help is better than no help, I must dispel and refute the belief that once an addict (or once an alcoholic), always an addict. If what you think and say you are is true, then why would I want to continually go around like people from NA and AA saying "Hi, I'm Ray, and I'm an addict" when I haven't used in years. Yes, in the beginning, seeing yourself and accepting who and what you are is important, but the reason I emphasize that our program and the best programs are spiritually based is because when you accept Jesus, He changes your "nature" and old things are gone. Therefore, I am not an addict anymore. I used to be. I once was, but now I am a new person. Now, I am a preacher, a pastor, a director, a husband, and a father, but I am not an addict. However, if I were to return to using, then I turn back to my old nature and again become the addict, but as long as I continue on this new path, I am a new creation in Christ Jesus (2 Corinthians 5:17).

Christian-based programs that emphasize a personal relationship with Christ, a disciplined lifestyle, and an understanding of one's addiction have proven to be the best programs for full recovery and healing of the addict. When I went away to the Christian program, God told me in the beginning that I was healed from drugs. He told me that I would never do drugs again, and since that time, I have always said in relationship to using again, "God won't do it, and the devil can't do it because the devil ain't devil enough because God has totally set me free." The Bible declares that "If the Son shall make you free, ye shall be free indeed" (St. John 8:36).

The spiritual programs give men a completely new life and not just a temporary makeover. Anyone ministering to those whose lives are ill-affected by drug addiction must realize that this is a spiritual fight as well as a natural one, probably more spiritual than natural because sin is the ultimate root problem. The battle must be won from the inside out. Remember Jesus and the "lunatic" man in the tombs (Mark 5). Most people were content to just have the lunatic out of the way. Put him up in a graveyard somewhere out of sight, out of mind. They were happy to leave him tied up and hurting. That is the way our society, for the most part, has dealt with the drug addicts. Put them up somewhere. Lock them up. Throw them in a thirty-day program or lock them up in jail. We don't want to see or face this ugliness, and I must say that society has not changed. For the most part, this attitude is unacceptable. Most people just look and walk on by or want to lock the person up and throw away the key. Maybe for some jail is the answer, but even then the problem won't just go away. It will touch our lives sooner or later. It will touch our homes, our children, our spouses, and our loved ones sooner or later, just like this man didn't go away. Day and night, he was crying and cutting himself. People heard, but they walked on by, leaving him crying, but he didn't want to be where he was, leaving him cutting and hurting himself continually because he couldn't stop. But he ran to Jesus and fell down before him, and Jesus saw what was on the inside of this man. Jesus saw his pain. Jesus knew he needed healing and deliverance from those demons that tormented him. The Lord understood that no one in their right mind wants to be in a graveyard cutting themselves, but this man was bound by Satan. He didn't just have an issue or mere problem, but Jesus came, Jesus saw, and Jesus set him free. Not just free from the graveyard, not just free from the cutting, but free from the inside out, totally free from his bondage. Many drug addicts and alcoholics are crying on the inside. They don't want to keep hurting themselves, but they are bound. They are crying, "What's wrong with me? Why do I keep hurting myself, my loved ones? I've lost everything and I still can't stop. Somebody help me."

This is the time that we must, with love, power, and wisdom, reach out and let them know that we understand and that there is someone greater than us that feels their every hurt, pain, desire, and longing, and He has come to set them free from the inside out (John 10:10, Luke 4:18). If we would only look. Look in our schoolhouses; there is someone still crying. Look in our neighborhoods; there is someone still crying. Look in our churches; there is someone still crying. And yes, look in our homes; there is someone still crying. We must hear the cry. We must stop the bleeding. Incarceration is an answer, but not the best answer for all. There are many that want and can be rehabilitated when placed in the right programs. Parents, society, churches, we can no longer afford to look the other way. Looking the other way might cause us to lose someone we love and care about.

In regard to those that may be trying to help their loved ones or those that are doing drug ministry, you have to consider if you are in or out of your lane. Whether you're helping a loved one or working in drug ministry, the old saying still applies: "You need to lead, follow, or get the heck out of the way." By following, I mean following someone that knows what they are doing. I know something about children and taking care of them, having raised a baby girl while on drugs as a single parent, but this does not necessarily qualify me to work in children's ministry because there is a lot about children's ministry that I don't know.

First and foremost, it is not where God placed me. I have good ideals and could help out, but to try and lead this ministry would be out of my lane. Those that are qualified and called to do ministry in any area must be able to find themselves in Mark 16: 17-18 and James 5:13-17, where there are signs that follow those that are qualified. In James, we see the initiative lies with the sick person having faith in God's healing power. Believing that the elders have the qualifications and the power that would characterize them as men of personal uprightness and spiritual maturity. Thus giving them special ability because of a real relationship with God to minister to those who are sick, men totally sold out to and for God with unwavering faith that when they prayed, God would move. Acts 1:4-5, 8 says the following:

> And being assembled together with *them, He commanded them not to depart from Jerusalem, but to wait for the Promise of the Father,* "which," *He said,* "you have heard from Me; for John truly baptized with water, but *you shall be* baptized with the Holy Spirit not many days from now.

> *But you shall receive power when the Holy Spirit has come upon you; and you shall be witnesses to me in Jerusalem, and in all Judea and Samaria, and to the end of the earth.*

You cannot do what you are not qualified to do. When I say "not qualified," this does not mean that you cannot get qualified for your particular ministry, but you must understand your calling, be trained to walk in your calling, and then walk in it with the anointing, but in your lane. How many people, for the sake of their families, knowing only bits and pieces about taxes, try to file their taxes themselves? Not many. So it is with ministry. We must operate in power in the area that God called us to. That is where we will be most effective, and in drug ministry, we cannot and will not do an effective work if we do not understand the altering that has taken place in the mind of those we are ministering to.

I wrote this book after being addicted to drugs for over twenty-seven years, after wasting and losing over half a million dollars. I know that when dealing with addicts and alcoholics, knowledge and understanding is power. When ministering to those who are addicted, you must realize that there are some who are not ready to stop because they are okay with the way life is. At the present time, they have no fear of God, feel they have no need for God, nor do they have a longing for a better life. This is where they want to be in life right now, thinking that they are cool, carefree, doing what they want.

Most addicts are addicted to the lifestyle as well as the drugs. They love the life they are living, so they live the life they love. We must be able to identify with the person standing before us—lost, confused, and addicted. We must be able to bring them to a place of understanding of themselves. Make them see who they have become. Make them see what they have lost. Make them see what awaits them if they continue on the path that they are on. Once we have their attention through prayer, discernment, and the power of God's Spirit, we must lead them to a course of healing and deliverance.

We must help them to understand their true root problem. We must make them understand what made them turn to drugs in the first place. What is the bandage of drug addiction covering? What is their real problem? The power of God wants to dig deep and bring out the root problems in these individual's lives so they can truly lead a free and victorious life. God wants to give them their right mind back and change them back to their real norm before drug addiction.

So what did I just say? We have to get them to first understand that they are bound and need to be free. Sometimes, we need to first get people to admit that they have a problem. People can be living such a messed-up life until they believe the lie that "things aren't that bad." Up until the day I left to get help, my daughter and I could not and would not have survived without living off others, but up until that day, I kept telling myself that "things aren't that bad."

Chapter Three

Desire and Control

James 1:12-15

There is a difference between desiring something and being controlled by that something you desire. Desire is a longing for something; it is a strong urge, but control is that which exercises authority over or has dominating influence over. It holds one in restraints. While I might desire to be rich and to have lots of money, I am not going to rob a bank, but the person who is obsessed and controlled by the desire to be rich has a stronghold over their life and is capable of getting a gun and committing robbery. I might long to have some ice cream, but because I am diabetic and want to live, I won't do it, but the person who is controlled by their desire will eat the ice cream, get sick, and go to the hospital; and if they keep eating the wrong things, they will die because the wrong foods have a stronghold over them. It is exercising control or authority over that person's desires. Thousands of people die every year because they are controlled by their desires and don't follow the doctor's orders. I have lost so many friends who knew that if they continued to drink, it would kill them, but guess what? They continued to drink and they died. Control!

Sometimes in the beginning, when a person tries drugs, it is just about their desire. Many individuals want to try it because someone, usually a so-called friend, says they should because it's cool. They tell them it won't hurt to just try it once to see what it is like. A lot of so-called friends do this because misery loves company. They are messed up and don't want you to live right. They feel like, why should you make it and they don't?

Then there are those who will hang with you and try to get you hooked because you have money, and if they get you hooked, then they can get high on your money. Many men feel that if they can get the women hooked, they can exchange sexual favors for drugs. For the majority, they like the way it makes them feel. For a moment in time, they can lose time and reality and "ride the mighty high"; but as they continue to indulge in this ecstasy, desire will turn to control and leave them out of control.

When the addict is being delivered in the beginning, he might still have a desire for drugs, but he must never again allow that desire to take control. He must fight temptation by and with the strength of Christ (1 Corinthians 10:13) until there is no longer even a hint of desire or longing for drugs. The Bible says in Romans 6:16, "To whom you yield yourself servants to obey his servants you become." The more the recovering addict yields to the newfound principles of life found in a relationship with Christ, the more they participate in a church ministry for those addicted or go through a Christian rehabilitation program and daily practice and participation in this new life, the more the stronghold of drugs will loosen, and the desire for drugs will disappear. Remember, a long tedious journey begins with the first step. You must start somewhere and be determined to finish. When drugs had me torn up from the floor up, well into the second year of my cocaine addiction, I had a run-in with Jesus Christ. Things had gotten real bad, and I had sold my van. He told me I needed to come back to where I should have always been. So I did. I went back to the church, but I knew I wasn't ready to be saved or give up certain things, yet I took a step closer to that direction. I kept coming to church knowing I wasn't there yet, but I came. I wasn't in the choir or on the deacon board, but I came. Hung over, suffering the effects of the weekend high, I came because I knew I was sick, and church is supposed to be the sinner's hospital. I sat in church week after week, heard the Word, the songs, and the testimonies. and little by little, they got me to the point where I became serious. It took some years, but I didn't give up. I wasn't healed at five hundred steps in my thousand-step journey, but my first step helped me get to my final step of being healed, delivered, and set free.

I believe that drugs (illegal and misused legal ones) in most cases are a kind of witchcraft. The word "witchcraft" in Hebrew comes from the word *pharnakos* or *pharmakia*, which is the root word of "pharmacy." Sorcery or witchcraft implies the "mixing of potions and the casting of spells." A great example is that of the coca plant. You take the leaf that is made into a paste that is made into a powder, then that powder which is cocaine is put into a tube with baking soda and water, mixed over fire, and stirred to make a "rock of cocaine." This rock is given to an individual who smokes it, or others just shoot up the powder by placing it in a spoon with water and cooking it with fire underneath the spoon, which turns it back into a liquid that they can shoot up. From that point, a spell is cast that most times causes a lifetime of heartaches. All this from a plant? Go figure. Who would have thought it? What human being, even with a crazy high IQ, could have come up with all this? No, Satan's DNA, his MO, is all over this one.

I believe that drug addiction is a means by which Satan gains control over the life of an individual and then works his hidden purpose through desire and control to bring total destruction. Drugs affect not only the individual's life but also the lives of their family, the coworker, the consumer, and society at large. Drugs are a surface problem that are so devastating, so controlling that you can't just get past it to get to your root problem. Satan won't let you face your root problems. You just keep self-medicating by getting high. He's in control, using desire to keep you bound. The real issues are your root problems, such as low self-esteem, sexual immorality, peer pressure, pride, a bad marriage, feelings of inadequacy as a parent, etc. but you are so controlled by and bewitched by the effects and desire of the drugs, you can't deal with these issues, which will—most of the time, once dealt with—help you to overcome your drug addiction when you face them head-on and overcome them by the power of Christ. Most of the time, drugs are used as a sedative, as a pain medication, as an escape from the real world; but in order to overcome and regain control of your life, you must deal with the desire and control factor.

In my early years, I wanted to be like Fredrick Douglass, W. E. B. Du Bois, someone famous in black history. At the end of my story, I wanted to be named among the great black intellectuals and inventors. That was my heartbeat, what made me tick. At the same time period, I knew I could also play major league sports. I had all the talent. I wanted to be a ballplayer. But I also wanted to be cool and bad for so long because I resented my ugly self and my square image. Thus, a new desire came, which took control. Like so many men in my age group, I read this book that glorified drugs, sex, and the hard-core party life. In the beginning, I had always resented drug dealers, pimps, and tough guys because remember, my desire was to be, as I stated, like Fredrick Douglas and the other historic black role models or play ball and be in the major league. But while reading the book, I never admitted to myself that the season in my life had changed and that I really secretly wanted to be somewhat like the character in the book. Most of us fellas wanted to be the player type of guy and not the pimp. I never owned up to the truth of how I had changed, and in the beginning, I only went so far in trying to be in that negative lifestyle, but eventually, I crossed the line. Always wanting to be cool for so long, resenting my ugly self, I bought into the negativity that was presented to me, my dark skin, broad Negro features, bad hair, and square image. I bought into the kids teasing and talking about me. Kids can be so cruel.

This new desire controlled me, and if truth be told, a lot of guys that read that book fell victim to the same desire and control. If they didn't get it from there, they got the attitude from someone or somewhere else—from their family, their friends, or their neighborhoods. While in ministry school, we were taught that television, movies, music, and the new wave of videos could be a part of the sewer lines that lead to America's living room. If we are what we eat, then are we not also whatever we take in? Some have the same desire to be the dope man as I had to be the player/lover. Some thought it was cool to be on drugs just like I thought it was cool to be the player/lover. I realized by 1978 how many women really wanted to be the baddest whores on the streets, cool, sexy, and using drugs. This was a change from the sixties. It was 1983, and I remember getting women for the white guys I was in construction with. I was talking with this one lady who was a schoolteacher. We were friends and could openly talk to each other. As I told her about what I was doing, out of the blue, she blew my mind. She asked if she could meet some of the guys because she had always wanted to live that type of life. Desire! Control! She was not on drugs and didn't look the part. She was a nice-looking white lady from the suburbs. I said I was doing it because I needed the money, but really, I could have done other things for the money. I wanted to feel cool 'cause on the inside, this was who I really wanted to be. Oftentimes, when in this negative lifestyle, we are actually doing things because we're looking to get the accolades from the in crowd, just living for the hype; but after a while, who remembers? Who cares! After a while, desire turned to control.

Let me give you some prime examples of movies and images put before us that changed our times and values. During the time of the civil rights era, the times of Medgar Evers, Malcolm X, and Dr. King, there was a mind-set in my community and many other communities of black pride.

James Brown said it best for us with his implementation of "Say It Loud—I'm Black and I'm Proud." Even though we were getting high at the time, we would sit and talk about overcoming segregation and how we would become somebody one day, along with these great leaders. During this time period, when driving down the street, if you saw a brother walking in your direction, it was a common practice to pull over and say, "What up, brother man, you need a ride?" Once in the car, usually the conversation, even if they had a joint in their hands, was about overcoming and being like the positive black role models. Back then, even if you got into a fight, his friends and your friends all stood around and made sure it was a fair fight; no one else jumped in. When it was over, usually the two of you forgot about it and went out and got a drink. Today, when brother man slows down in his car, you run for your very life because movies, music, and videos say it is cool to kill your brother based on what color he is wearing or because he is not from your part of the hood.

And then it happened. King was assassinated—our positive image, our role model, our leader was removed from us, and no one took his place that could captivate the minds of the people. Instead, what happened was we finally started getting black movies, which we had never had, and although they helped propel some African Americans' careers, the imagery of these movies tore down so much of what we had before King's death. The movies started with *Sweet Sweetback's Baad Song*, *Shaft*, *Super Fly*, *The Mack*, and the list goes on. Within a short period of time, at least in Milwaukee, so many had converted their Cadillac to a pimp mobile. Grill in the front, diamond in the back, sunroof top. You know the deal. They wore the long leather and fur coats for men and the extremely large wide-rim hats. All of a sudden, the new image in the inner city was no longer that of a young man talking about being a positive black role model or about how we could become a proud black community, but now, in order to be the so-called accepted cool guy, you had to be the pimp, the player, the dope dealer, or the stickup man.

This can not be applied to everyone in the community because many were strong enough to maintain their integrity, and my hat is off to them because there were many who just didn't "go there" regardless of what everybody else was doing. Today, I really respect my brothers and sisters who held out, no matter how people considered them to be "the square from nowhere." For them to have more pride in who they knew they were and the positive person they wanted to become versus being so-called cool is a sign of ultimate strength.

I can remember watching one of today's African American divas doing some type of benefit concert for children. As I watched her perform, I felt her performance was too "nasty," too provocative for her audience. Her audience was young African American girls that were under the age of twelve. Girls that are at an impressionable age. There was too much hip swinging, and her attire was too much of the "miss thing" image. The camera showed one young girl that appeared to be hypnotized with so much admiration for the performer. I could only wonder as to how she was relating to this image before her. What was her dream, her fantasy at this time? We have to be careful of what we portray, that it does not become borderline promiscuity because in all that we do, we are actually selling a product, and we never want to create a negative image because images can become desires, and some desires can become controlling.

Chapter Four

Root Problems

Proverbs 24:10; Romans 7:14-25

As stated before, some root problems are peer pressure, sexual immorality, low self-esteem, molestation, pride, stubbornness, poverty, and the list goes on. These can lead a person to drugs and alcohol. For me, these six things in this order were my root problems. When I was about seven years old, two older girls took me in the closet and sexually molested me. We went for it. They were eleven and thirteen. In 1958, kids didn't know then what kids know today at these same ages about life and sex. Never would I have tried to initiate this on my own. In 2006, while painting the offices of a well-known psychiatrist in Chicago, we had a talk about my addiction to sex that I had experienced throughout my life. Help me, Jesus. Oh, God. She told me that my little young mind had no chance to process what had happened to me in that closet, and therein was the monster created. She had studied, analyzed, and learned a lot about Christian leaders in ministry with sexual problems. Most of her practice was along this line—dealing with leaders in the church that had sexual addictions. She knew her stuff, but here is what I believe. Although she was exactly right in her diagnosis, I believe that the monster (sex addict) was lying dormant in me for a long time until it was activated by peer pressure. The monster was alive and raging on the inside, but the calm nature of who I was supposed to be kept him in check. The monster was always looking for a way out. In front of him were Malcolm and Martin and the men I most admired and wanted to be like. I fantasized about feeding the masses, giving away homes to the needy, and just being a do-gooder on the world scene, but not as a preacher. I did not want to be some goody-two-shoes preacher like the kids were starting to call me around the age of eight or nine. I just wanted a wife, four kids, the ability to be able to do for others, and to go down in black history as somebody, but I loved sin more than God or my dreams (St. John 14:21, 23; 1 John 2:15-17). So here is how it went.

I craved sex like any other young person. Around twelve years old, I wanted to be sexually active, but in the beginning, it wasn't easy for me to be sexually active, and I was able to deal with it. I really wanted to express sexual desires, but I was okay, although I would try whenever I thought I had a chance. I would look for chances. Sometimes, I would go a year without having sex. A lot of us young guys between the ages of twelve and sixteen lied about having sex and the frequency thereof. So although I was not sexually active like I wanted, I was okay. It was a little hard, but I wasn't about to lose my mind over it—a little sleep, but not my mind. Understand what I am saying here. I had an issue! An issue with sex, which was very prevalent in my mind. I would sit and daydream about it even if at that time I didn't go out of my way to fulfill it. This, for me was a root problem, and because of my totally sold-out nature and weakness to be like the so-called cool guys and fit in with the crowd, I started to try harder to be and do things that were not really me. Peer pressure drove me harder and further than my desire for sex. I had no control. My wanting to be in the "in crowd" led me to the wrong crowd. If I wanted to be cool and have sex with the girls, I had to hang around the crowd that was drinking, getting high, and going to the parties. So instead of going to school at fourteen and fifteen, half the time I was somewhere drinking, smoking, getting high, and searching for a girl that would have sex with me. Not just any girl, because there were plenty of what we called square or lame girls that would have gladly had sex with me, but I had to have one that was in the in crowd because I wanted to be in the in crowd, the party crowd, the right crowd, or, should I say, the wrong crowd. I needed the accolades, the hype of being cool, being one of the guys.

That's peer pressure. That's what it was all about. Thus, peer pressure drove me from my desire to be like Malcolm and Martin to desiring to be like the well-groomed ladies' man, the partier, the player instead of the businessman. It drove me from my desire to be like Fredrick Douglas, W. E. B. Du Bois, Booker T. Washington, Babe Ruth, Hank Aaron, and Jim Brown. A desire, which on a scale of one to ten was a twelve, changed because negative influence driven by peer pressure—which on a scale of one to ten was about a fifteen—was greater and more domineering. I traded a good peer group for a bad one. I would often sit and wonder where I would be today had I been man enough to hold on and follow my true dreams. When that strong man of sexual addiction stemming from my sexual molestation joined the strong man of peer pressure, wanting to be cool and down with the in crowd, those two monsters together created the strong man that destroyed my life. Now my freak nature escalated, driven by an overwhelming desire for sex combined with wanting to be cool and accepted, and it held me in bondage for the next thirty years. Oh, my God! Oh, my God! Thank you, Jesus, for the twins, grace and mercy.

Once I learned the Word of God, I understood what happened. Ephesians 6:12 says, "For our struggle is not against flesh and blood, but against the rulers, against the authorities, against the powers of this dark world and against the spiritual forces of evil in the heavenly realms." Daniel 10:12-13 states, "Then he said to me, 'Do not fear, Daniel, for from the first day that you set your heart to understand, and to humble yourself before your God, your words were heard; and I have come because of your words. But the prince of the kingdom of Persia withstood me twenty-one days; and behold, Michael, one of the chief princes, came to help me, for I had been left alone there with the kings of Persia.'" Daniel 10:12-13 backs up Ephesians 6:12. There is a force beyond us, stronger than us, that is fighting us, a force that if the angels needed help to defeat, then what about us?

I was raised in the church, came from a long line of presiding elders and pastors. I did in church just what I did in junior high and high school. Nothing! I lived in my own little world until about eleven, and then by twelve, I was starting to look around, checking life out, and by thirteen, that damned monster was kicking at the door of my mind, emotions, and will. My spirit was not strong enough to even be called weak. I had no relationship with God, no knowledge of His Word, and I didn't even realize that I had a spirit. So because I didn't know anything about the principalities, the rulers of darkness of this world, the spiritual host of wickedness in the heavenly places, how could I fight? I was trying to fight in my own strength. I was trying to fight that guy in the red union underwear with the pitchfork in his hand. You know the one with the long tail. Little did I know that Satan had been an angel in charge of praise and worship, and when he got the boot in the butt, he had already conned one-third of the angels. If he could con the angels, who are we for him to defeat if we are not living for God?

Satan is the prince of the air for right now until Jesus Christ comes back to claim His own. Satan has folks, and they have clearly defined roles and levels of authority in a real though invisible sphere of activity. Satan has some power; otherwise, Jesus would not have said what he did in Luke 10:19: "Behold, I give you the authority to trample on serpents and scorpions, and over all the power of the enemy, and nothing shall by any means hurt you." Thank God, Jesus has all power. Praise Him! The power He gave the twelve and the seventy in Luke 9:1 and Luke 10:1 he also promised to us. Acts 1:8 (KJV) says, "But you shall receive power when the Holy Spirit has come upon you; and you shall be witnesses to me in Jerusalem, and in all Judea and Samaria, and to the end of the earth." This scripture lets us know that the power of the Holy Ghost is for us to be able to live right and serve. But you cannot even get the power of the Holy Ghost if you are not saved. Little did I know before getting saved for real that when I asked God to forgive me for what I had done, even though in my heart I knew that I intended to go right on doing it, that prayer bounced all around the room and never went past the ceiling. Jesus said in Luke 4:18, *"The Spirit of the LORD is upon me, because He has anointed me to preach the gospel to the poor; He has sent me to heal the brokenhearted, to proclaim liberty to the captives and recovery of sight to the blind, to set at liberty those who are oppressed."* This scripture plainly lets us know that Christ came to set us free, but because I had no sincere intentions of repenting, my prayer was not heard. Then in Psalms 66:18, the scriptures says, *"If I regard iniquity in my heart, the Lord will not hear."* I had not truly repented and was just like those individuals Jesus spoke of in Matthew 15: 7-9: *"Hypocrites! Well did Isaiah prophesy about you, saying: These people draw near to me with their mouth, and honor me with their lips, but their heart is far from me, and in vain they worship me, Teaching as doctrines the commandments of men."* Therefore, because I did not understand the Scriptures or true repentance, that monster Satan kicked my butt all over the place.

There was no way I could have held on to the good intensions I had in my heart as a young person, so I just thank God again for the twins, grace and mercy. The enemy has come to steal, kill, and destroy. Satan knows that if he can steal your dreams, your joy, your peace, and your focus, you will lower your guard, your standards, and do things you may not have given into if your standards had not been lowered. A person who has lost their joy, peace, or focus is a person without hope, a person void of life. Where there is no joy, no peace, no focus, there is no progression, no vision. When Satan steals any or all these things, we are dead men walking. Then there are those who do have joy, peace, and focus, but it is of the wrong source. It is worldly, and because it is worldly, then they can only look for and expect to get that joy, peace, and focus from those things that the world offers.

So many times later in my life, I would sit and think how, if I could, I would take back all the skipping school, drinking, smoking weed, stealing cars, going to the basement-quarter parties, trying to be cool, and all the other madness. I was an alcoholic by fifteen years old. Sometimes I didn't even remember where my classes were when I did go to school. I did so many crazy things from December 1966 unto September 1993 that I am so sorry about, but I talk about them now because I don't want anyone else to go through all the needless nonsense and hell that I went through. Another reason I admit to some of these embarrassing things I did is because I was so bad that some people still tie me to my childhood and young adult years. I guess when I'm in Milwaukee, it is easier to go ahead and talk about it because someone is always going to bring up something about the past anyways. Somebody has to crack a joke about me being drunk or me and the women every time I'm in town. I can't even count the costs for my foolish actions. It caused me to lose one of my childhood friends. He will talk to me when I see him but will not return any calls. That will hurt for the rest of my life. Thank God I still have Larry Carr. Love you, bro. Carl Lenoir, where are you?

I was in Milwaukee in January 2010, and someone brought up how my cousin Sideena had to pull me from a snowbank where I had fallen out "drunk as a skunk." That happened in 1968! The saddest and the hardest thing for me is that at the end of having spent about half a million dollars and about forty years of hell, including my bad marriage, about 80 percent of the time, I was doing the things that *I really didn't want to be doing, and I didn't enjoy most of them. I was only trying to be cool.* I had become addicted to the lifestyle. So many things I did over the years I could not stop doing because I didn't know anything else. I didn't know any other life. Because of my choices, life has been hard. About 80 percent of my education came after the age of twenty-four. I had to educate myself because I played the fool in school.

Some people are driven to drugs out of curiosity. The more they are told to stay away, the more they hear about certain things, the more they want to see what the hype is all about. Some feel that they can handle it, that they won't get hooked, and that they can handle seeing what it is all about. In other words, some people are so nosy—oops, I mean they have such a problem with curiosity—that they stay in some kind of mess. Some church kids are notorious for this problem. Raised in perceived good Christian homes, they can't wait until they are eighteen or twenty-one to get out of the house and do their own thing. Their own thing too often will lead them to the wrong man, wrong woman, and wrong source of pleasure. Too often it leads them to the arms of drug addiction, whether a person's initial problem is a false sense of self-pride, peer pressure, wanting to be accepted by the crowd, or perhaps a person is just curious about how the drug will make them feel. Perhaps they are sad and depressed and just need a pick-me-up because so many children in the pastor's house and in the believer's house have had so little excitement compared to worldly stimulation until they can't wait to get out the house and try what they perceive to be "fun stuff." I'm not saying that they should be allowed to indulge and try things in the world, but what I am saying is that if you're going to keep them away from the evils of the world, expose them to the good stimulation outside of church so they are well cultivated and learned. They need to have stimulation outside of just bowling, skating, movies, or going to the restaurants. These things are good, but we just need to broaden the horizon for our children to keep them excited about good, wholesome Christian living. One thing is for sure: however a person gets to drugs, I believe it is linked to their root problem, whether in church or out of church.

Whatever the circumstances are that gets one involved with drugs, it is all related to the sin nature. That nature that wants to always go contrary to the things of God, that nature that always wants to follow the easy ways that leads to destruction. That nature that will always look for the way that seems right unto man but the end thereof is the way of death. If a person does not overcome their drug addiction, their way will eventually lead to death because drugs will always eventually get the best of all who travel the road of "desire," which will only lead to "control." In the beginning, you reached for it; but in the end, it comes for you. It controls you. Satan will set you up before time so that when the time comes for you to get the blessings of God, Satan has a hook in you and it won't let you go (Acts 8:9-12). I've talked with a number of women who were on drugs, whoring around, not taking care of their children. They were just out there in the streets, living bad and looking bad. After spending many hours of ministering with these women, I have found that many have similar stories. Their story begins like this: "My mother was not there for me like a real mother! She only provided the necessities of life. I never received her love, affection, and attention. She only gave those things necessary for me to live. I never had a mother's love." The real bad ones would say that their mother was a crack whore living crazy and never took care of them. They had to be raised by their grandmother. Now they were living the same life. Most of these women started doing things trying to get their mother's love and attention. They yielded to the peer pressures, hung out with the wrong crowds, started sleeping around, drinking, and then drugs. Thus, a part of their root problems was jealousy and anger. That anger was directed toward the world, at anybody and everybody, but it was really because of the lack of love from their mothers. They find themselves in the same lifestyle, their anger intensified as their mother's love (the mother who neglected them) was turned toward the grandchild they were now taking care of because the daughter had become just like or worse than the mother had been. As a matter of fact, the women were actually worse than their mother had been because they were not even providing the basic necessities for their own children.

Then there are others who are the oldest child in the family; their mother had them as a teenager. They didn't get the love and affection, so they rebelled, went out, and got involved with the wrong crowd—the in crowd—and ended up on drugs. They are now mad and rebellious because their mother had settled down, had more children, and she is giving them what she never gave the older child—a mother's love. These women were busy dealing with so many men in the faces of their children that there was no room left to love their children. There is no way they can work on all these issues, their root problems, when their lives are totally controlled by drugs. Until they can get past their surface problems of drug addiction, they cannot deal with their root problems of anger, jealousy, and lack of love and relationship with their mothers.

Therefore, it is essential that a person, when getting healed from drug or alcohol addiction, look deeper and get into the root causes for the real reason that they are out of control. When a person gets off drugs, they can still have a host of other issues—sin issues or life issues—to deal with. So if we can get rid of the sin issues, overcome the life issues, all while we're getting over the drug issues, we can walk a glorious and victorious life. Remember, John 8:36 tells us, "If the Son shall make you free, you shall be free in deed." We often misquote this scripture, stating, "If the Son shall set you free," but anything that can be set free can be recaptured or imprisoned again. However, "If the Son shall make you free" infers completeness and wholeness. When we completely submit our lives to the Lord, He creates or makes us into a new person totally and completely. Therefore, we are not just set free for a time to be locked up again, but we are made forever into another person that is healed and delivered as long as we continue in the new path that he sets us on.

Chapter Five

Owning Up to "Satan Is Pimping Me"

John 10:10; John 8:44

Admitting that you are hooked, strung out, or addicted is just not enough. It is the starting point, the beginning. It is not enough to say "I'm addicted to drugs." You must understand the nature and ugliness of your addiction. A person must realize that Satan is treating them just as any pimp treats his whore. When a whore is sent out to work, she makes the money and must bring it all back to the pimp. She gets very little out of the deal. A so-called good pimp will make sure his whores have some clothes, a place to stay, and food to eat. She must look good and have strength to work. Yeah, you've probably guessed where I'm going with this. Satan does not care if you have food, clothes, a place to stay, or anything else because he knows that he has you hooked and you're always going to bring everything back to him. All your money, all your time, and all your dreams are wasted in him. For many, just like a good pimp who tries to keep his whores feeling as though there is nothing wrong with what they are doing, Satan makes you feel that what you are doing is not really bad. The whores and the prostitutes think they are just offering a commodity. Satan's big lie says, "You're gonna give it away, so why not make some money while doing it?" Satan tells our young people that they are hip; everyone else is square. "You are going to make money, big money. Everyone else is working these little chump jobs," he says. The devil with his witchcraft says, "Go ahead, just sit back and enjoy life, feel good, make money, ride this mighty high. Drive your fast hyped-up cars, flash your cash, sport your fancy clothes. You've got it going on." Before the devil takes you down, he tries to convince you that you're okay. Sometimes you're paying your bills; you're taking care of your family somewhat. The devil tries to convince you that things are not as bad as they really seem. He says, "It's okay to use drugs. You ain't hurting nobody. It's okay to sell them. People are going to buy them from somebody."

Then there are the old sob stories. Satan really gets many of us with these lies. The lie that says, "Because I was born poor, in the ghetto, lived in the projects, didn't have the opportunities that others had, this is my way out." Some say, "Because my parents lived this way and never showed me better, this is all I know." Others buy into the lies that are said about them—"You'll never be anybody, you'll never amount to anything"—so they just end up with a self-fulfilled prophecy. They feel this is the way their life is supposed to be. "I'll make something out of myself with the money, and then I'll stop." Satan is saying, "You trick!" In America, Satan has used the media industry to promote his wicked, evil, and destructive agenda. Many movies, songs, Internet sites, and magazines promote immorality at its finest, making it easy to sink into a pit of sin and darkness. Thus, many individuals become so caught up in the sin life that includes X-rated movies, gangster rap, hard-core acid rock music, whoredom, the cool gangster and playboy images so that they cannot see their bondage. They see the killing and the dying around them, people going to prison for long periods of time, but the devil tells them, "It will never happen to you. You've got your stuff all together. Drugs will never overcome or control you. Your will is too strong." Until people wake up and stop letting Satan pimp them, until they realize that they are not in control but the enemy is, they will keep going down a slippery slope. They must realize, like the song says, "I'm on the highway to hell."

Then there are those who have come to the point where they realize that they have lost control. They realize that they are in bondage, but they still are not at the point where they want to stop. Many knew ten, twenty years ago that they were no longer in control, but they were not ready to change because they still enjoyed the high, still enjoyed chasing the high. They still do not see the wrong in what they are doing. Satan is still in control in the driver's seat. He has tricked you to get that control, and he will do whatever is necessary to keep it: feed you any old lie or take you into a thirty-day program that will only give you a break but no deliverance. He still holds the reins; he just makes you stable for a moment to give you a little rest. Satan relishes in the control that he gets over our lives when we are addicted. He leads by strong-arm tactics. God leads us by our spirit because our wills are submitted to Him. God leads us because we want to be led. "The Lord is my Shepherd." He is mine because I make Him mine. It is not force, but choice. Reverend Carpenter taught me over and over again the following: God is a spirit, and He leads us by His Spirit. His Spirit leads our spirit. He does not lead us by our soul, which is mind, emotion, and will. Our spirit is intuition, communion, and conscience with God. So if your soul is in control, then obviously, your spirit is not in control. We often say that we need to crucify our flesh, kill it; we don't actually mean that we should kill it, but rather subdue it and bring it into subjection to the leading of our spirit because we definitely need the attributes of our soul to aid and support our spirit.

Satan controls and leads by force. Back in the day, we would say that there were two kinds of pimps—one being a smooth-talking ladies' man, and the other was what was called a gorilla pimp. He tried to force women to work for him. Both are ugly, but Satan is that gorilla pimp. If you let the devil ride, sooner or later, he's gonna try to drive. Once he gets his hooks in, he dares you to move any way but the way he is pulling. If your flesh (soul) is in control, then Satan is in control. If your spirit is submitted to God, then God is in control and will lead your spirit. When man does not have a godly conscience, then there is no limit to the ungodly things he will do. What is it that makes a man or woman steal everything out of the home of their struggling aged parent and sell it on the streets for drugs? What is it that makes a man take the rent money when his wife and children are about to be set out on the streets just to get drugs? What is it that makes a person put a gun to his best friend's head for a ten-dollar rock? It is that fleshy man being controlled by Satan, the master, that his will is submitted to. No matter how sorry you are, you cannot just quit because Satan is your pimp. He pulls your chain; you respond. You must find the Lord that is greater than him. You must want to be free from his pimp mentality. Satan is a strong man, and as long as we serve Satan, have his mind, sit and be controlled by him, we cannot cast him out (Matthew 12:25-30).

The prodigal son in Luke 15:11-32 wised up to Satan pimping him. He realized that the devil had sent him to work to get his inheritance and caused him to spend it on worldly living, and then Satan tried to break and destroy him with sorrow. He had to "own up" to Satan being in control and pimping his every move. Are there any tricks in the house? It is so sad to think that so many women feel like they are handling their business 'cause they go out and sell their bodies, usually for ten to twenty dollars for the most part, in the inner city. I don't want to gross anyone out by telling what most men ask them to do for that ten or twenty dollars. The woman goes and brags about how she just caught a trick, but then she goes and gives that same money to the dope man for a ten-minute high. Who's the real trick? Ninety-nine percent of the time, most of them come home with nothing for the house or the kids; not that this would justify what she did. Back in the day, street slang said, "It's a poor whore that can't even make it home with a loaf of bread." What I am saying is that as long as we allow Satan to be in control, he will pimp us with no shame. I know in the streets we always said, "Ain't nobody pimping me. Ain't nobody punking me out, I'm my own man [or woman]. I'm not going out like that." But you really are. Whether you admit it or not, Satan is in control. He is your lord, and he is pimping you. Remember what the Bible says in Romans 6:16, "Do you not know that to whom you present yourselves slaves to obey, you are that one's slaves whom you obey, whether of sin leading to death, or of obedience leading to righteousness?" Only by submitting your will and spirit to Christ Jesus will every yoke be broken and Satan's stronghold be defeated.

Chapter Six

The Enabler

1 Samuel 3:11-14, 4:12-18

We understand that an "enabler" is one whose behavior will allow another person to continue in a self-destructive pattern by providing excuses and means for them to not deal with the consequences of their actions or behaviors.

Most of the time, the enabler is a codependent in a dysfunctional relationship—mothers and children, husbands and wives, boyfriends and girlfriends. Those in this codependent relationship are manipulated by the life of the addict to the point that they hamper their recovery.

For example, parents and spouses often keep providing the addicted person with money in response to their lies of not getting their checks or losing their jobs and saying it wasn't their fault. They lie to bosses and coworkers, pastors, and friends for the addicted dependent. This codependent or enabler's behavior will not allow the addict to reach the point of hopelessness, helplessness, and brokenness that will cause them to reach out for help because they continue to provide for and make excuses for them. Been there, done that, ouch, amen. I paid a horrific price for being a codependent.

Before I went away to get off drugs, I went to my niece's graduation from the same Christian program I eventually went to. She had talked to the staff about me being a minister who had relapsed. The staff had talked with the director and gotten it approved for me to stay without going through the regular channels that was necessary until later (God will make a way). I told them if I stayed, I would be saying to myself that I wasn't man enough to stop on my own. Hahahaha. Anyway, I didn't stay. This was in April, and I met the person who would become my first wife in June. Had I stayed in the ministry program in April, I never would have met her in June.

Although I started out as an enabler, I later became her mentor. When I was living right and walking right before God, I had a witness within myself; well, after our sexual sin that is. After we had committed fornication, I sat and cried like a baby then repented and got back up and on track. I was able to uplift her, teach her, and encourage her to do the right things. But the end did not justify the means because I went through pure hell laboring with her, crying, devastated through the hurt and pain. All the time praying, trying to get her to see her sin, to see herself, and to come to a place of righteousness where she could see herself being an awesome woman of God. My life and my calling was put on hold through the process. When we met, she knew nothing about God or the Word of God at all. Eventually, the witness made a difference because she did get clean and saved for over three years. There was even a period when I was presiding as chief elder where I was allowed to let her teach Sunday school and Bible study, which she was great at. She was definitely called and had such a heart for ministry, but I felt that she had demons working overtime to pull her back. It was as though she had a dual personality. One moment she was fighting with all her heart to save her marriage and do ministry, and the next moment those demons would overpower her and she would be caught up again in the hard places. Along the way, she taught me a lot about having a true burden for ministry. I have learned so much from so many.

Although she eventually went back, what God used me to put in her was a sure foundation in His Word that is able to turn her around again, and I hope it does one day. The twins, God's grace and mercy, had given me the strength to mentor her through her addiction and numerous adulterous affairs without falling myself, but when she went back after three years, I was done because there was no more mentoring to be done, no more teaching to be taught. I was not going to be consumed with being an enabler all over again. She gave me a notarized statement made out to the Circuit Court of Illinois admitting her adultery so that I could get divorced and go on with my life and my ministry because regardless of what she did, I know in her heart she really did love me and the ministry. However, because she had never really dealt with her root problems, she continued to return to her surface problems and could never reach that place in her life where she could pursue a dedicated life in ministry.

Remember, as I stated before, enablers are oftentimes parents, spouses, siblings, or friends. I'm a mama's boy and I loved my mother. It is so true that "there is no love like a mother's love." No love is greater other than the love of Jesus. That being said, let me step in the mud. There is no enabler like a mother. If a mother is an enabler, oftentimes, they do the wrong things out of pure love and lack of knowledge. Mama may feel that if "I just give them the money, they won't have to do a crime to get it. If I just allow them to live at home, then they won't end up getting killed in the streets [although those that are grown should be on their own]." Mothers don't want to let their children "just die" without doing anything and everything they can to prevent death.

I had read a story about a mother lifting a heavy piece of farm equipment that had fallen on her child. It was reported that four men couldn't have lifted it, but this was the power of a mother's love, a mother who refused to just watch her son die. There are many such stories of mothers doing these miraculous, heroic things to save their children. Enablers mean only to help and not hurt. It is not their intention to make the problem worse, but there is a right way to do everything.

Proverbs 14:12 says, "There is a way which seemeth right unto a man, but the end thereof are the ways of death." Because the addict is not in his or her right mind and you want to help, you must first get an understanding and be informed about what you are trying to do (Proverbs 3:5,6). Let God lead you to someone that can help you and provide you with the knowledge of how you can help your loved one.

Drug addiction is no ordinary thing. It is complicated and a tremendous stronghold. I knew a mother that was a minister, and she told me that her only child was away in jail for about sixty days. She wanted me to minister to him because I had been where he was and had made it out. She wanted me to try and get him away from the mean streets of Chicago, away from the inner city and into a Christian rehabilitation housing ministry. The day before he was to get out of jail, she called and told me that since he had been away in jail for a while, they decided that the year-long program would be too long for them to be apart from each other. She said she now felt that she knew best how to handle her son. Well, she met him at the bus station and brought him home, and later on that evening, he went out. She called me the next day crying to let me know that he had been shot in the head and killed.

Then there was the mother who had tried everything in every way to help her daughter. After talking with the first lady of her church, she was told about my ministry. She called to ask if I could help her daughter. I told the mother not to tell her daughter that I was a minister but rather just a person that had been where she was. Sometimes people on drugs will not deal with someone that has not been on drugs or in that lifestyle. Some feel that all the preacher wants is another chance to preach at somebody. This grandmother was keeping her grandchildren all the time now and had put her daughter out. She would allow her to come to the house once a day for a meal, but when she put the last bite of food in her mouth, she had to go. This grandmother did well. She refused to watch her daughter die in front of her eyes. She took the grandchildren and got them in church. She talked to the first lady of the church about getting some help for her daughter.

That's where I came in. She did her best and sought God to do the rest. I can't effectively describe just how bad off this daughter really was. She was once a productive citizen with a good job, working in downtown Chicago. Let me just say that she was messed up, torn up from the floor up, but I was able to minister to her and get her to go to a Christian ministry in Michigan. She finished the year-long program, worked on staff, helping others for two years, then she left and got a job and got her kids back. Now she is a settled woman in church and raising her own kids because her mother decided to no longer be an enabler but to rather be proactive in saving her daughter from the highway of destruction.

In contrast, there was another mother who said that she loved her daughter who had gotten caught up in drug addiction, but she treated her daughter like pure hell, trying to use a tactic that would shame her daughter into changing. She would curse her to her face, call her derogatory names in front of her family and friends. This mother would tell her daughter's business at church to scandalize her name. She would call her daughter a whore and tell the granddaughter the things that her mother did with various men to discredit the mother. This mother treated and talked about her daughter like a dog but allowed her to stay in the home. The grandmother took over the raising of the granddaughter and has had her ever since, even to this day some twenty years later. This mother was an enabler for her own selfish gains, and the worst thing this daughter could have done was to stay around her mother only to be torn down.

She now has all kinds of mental and emotional problems, and so does the granddaughter. All three are totally messed up. This mother tried to shame her daughter into doing right, but she went about it in all the wrong ways. You must know what you are doing when you are ministering to those with addictions. Many individuals try to be a witness, telling others what to do and how to live right, when they are living like hell and don't even know the Word themselves.

When you are not living right, your witness is never effective. All the hurtful words and mistreatment from this mother made the daughter buy into the negativity and caused her to believe even more that she was inherently bad and that she wasn't anything just like what her mother said. Today, she suffers from low self-esteem, no confidence in herself, and no sense of self-pride, having bought into the lie that she will never change. For years she has allowed not only the drugs to ruin her, but also for men to mistreat her because she bought into her mother's lies when, in fact, the daughter had been an "A" student throughout most of her high school years—very intelligent, excellent with poetry, and gifted in song, totally confident and motivated.

I understand a mother saying, "I'm not just going to let my child die in the streets." But you must understand that you are allowing them to slowly die at home when you just let them stay at home, use drugs, and do nothing. When you continue to provide for the child and do nothing, you are allowing them to die. So what do you do when your loved one is out of their mind and out of control, headed for death, hell, and destruction? If you really want to help them, then you must get someone that understands the addict's mentality and someone who can lead them out of their wilderness of addiction and into a relationship with Christ. You must find someone who will locate the right ministry program that will lead them to the healing of God. If you are just allowing them to stay in their mess, you are not helping. Give them tender love and care, but also give them tough love that will help push them to make the right decisions. Let them know you have done all you can and that they now have to choose between right and wrong, between heaven and hell.

Mamas, you must decide what kind of help you will be—a real help, which means tough decisions, or an enabler. If you just sit and let them stay with you while doing nothing, you help them die slow; and if you just kick them out without pointing them in the right direction, then they could die fast. Get a plan. Point them in the right direction to receive help and stand your ground. Help them to recovery with tough love. I let people know that what sometimes works for one person may not work for another. Some people, if put out, could live in the streets until a change comes; others could not. You need to know your loved ones. Some need to go directly into a ministry program because they would die right away on the streets.

We want the blessing of God, but have we chosen God to be our God, to be our Lord, to be our all? (Joshua 24:13-16, Jeremiah 2:26-28, and Jeremiah 6:16). We want what we need from God, but are we giving God what He wants from us to do what we want done from Him? Are we living right? Are we in line with the Word to receive our blessings, or are we out of God's will? What time is it in our lives? Read Psalms 69:13 and Isaiah 49:8, 55:6. These scriptures tell us that there is a time when God is near; He is hearing us and about to heal, but we need to do our part so that God can bless us.

My dad was the type that when my daughter and I stayed with him and I would ask him for money, he would pat his pockets and say, "I think I got five dollars." However, before I got on drugs, he would say in his southern brawl, "Sho, sho, what you need?" He would give me two and three thousand dollars or more if I needed it because he knew I would pay him back. Once I was on drugs, he used to tell my sister how he felt about my staying with him all the time and not paying my way. He knew I would hear it from her, but what could I say? I couldn't pay because I was spending all my money on drugs. He would tell my sister, not that he was afraid of me, but because this was his way of venting and sending a message. He didn't like confrontation in light of his temper. He didn't want to physically hurt his son. So he sent the message without saying it directly to me, but he still let me and my baby stay, and we ate. He talked behind my back, knowing that if I said anything smart, he would go upside my head, kick me out, and keep my baby! He was seventy-nine during this time, and as much as he loved me, he let me know he still could go a round or two; and after that, he had the shotgun. He let me know that as much as he loved me, there were just certain things that I could not do in his house. I couldn't bring women, drugs, or other addicts over to where my dad lived, and believe me, I didn't even dare to do any of those things even when he was away fishing. I knew that his principles were as strong as his love, and if I made him, he would put me out. I had to respect his house.

I also remember when my sister would give me money whenever I asked. She would buy Easter, Christmas, and school clothes for my three kids. But when I didn't get any help to change my ways, she would tell me, "I'm going to stop helping." She kept helping for a while, and she would let me come to her house and eat. She would also babysit ReRe for me. I could come over, sleep, wash our clothes, and eat, but she would not give me a penny. Then whenever she let me stay, she would make me so uncomfortable to the point where I wished that I was somewhere else.

What she and my father made me realize when they stopped giving me money, when they made me think about my life, was that I could no longer say, "Well, if I spent all my money, I know my dad or sister will come through for me." When the well dried up and the money stopped, it slowly made a change in my life. The way my dad "shamed" me by talking about me to my sister worked in part because of who I was and the pride issues I had. It made me man up. It made me realize that I no longer wanted to be this same old person anymore. When they no longer enabled me, I was able to see how bad I needed help. At some point, mothers, fathers, spouses, children, and all loved ones need to stop making excuses for themselves and the addict. They need to stop being the enablers.

Mothers are many times the worst ones in this area, letting their grown children, thirty and forty years old, run in and out the house for years and decades. They take a little bit of money from the short jobs their children hold or from the SSI income check, money that is usually only enough to buy some food that the kids eat up while claiming that they let their son or daughter stay because they are paying their way. The cycle of putting them out for two weeks and letting them come back for two years continues until they both look up and they are almost too old to do anything else because life and time has passed them by. They wake up one day and realize they have wasted most of their lives. Oftentimes, mothers spend so much time fussing, even cursing, thinking that they are not an enabler because they tell their children off, set them straight so to speak. However, you have to realize that when you get finished raising hell and fussing, talking about what you're not going to allow in your house, that all you have done is fuss because you still allow your grown children to continue the cycle of running in and out of your house while still being addicted to drugs. So after twenty, thirty years, what's changed?

You know the old saying, "Lead, follow, or get the heck out of the way." Seeing as how you can't lead them and you're surely not going to follow them, you need to understand that you're in the way. Get upset with me if you will—that's fine—but get out of the way and get somebody in the situation that is qualified to do what you cannot do. If you would search for help as fervently as you argue and fuss, you would be doing much more for your loved one. And this also goes for the fathers, spouses, boyfriends, and girlfriends. Just like some love really ain't no love at all, sometimes some help really ain't no help at all. "Hey, where did everybody go? Is anybody listening?"

Chapter Seven

Caught Up the Hard Place

Psalms 19:14; James 4:17

Most of the time, there comes a point when a person really wants to be free. After years of going through pure hell, after years of hurting the people you love, after years of dodging death, you really want a way out. However, before you get free, you usually land in one more place—the hard place. At this place, it is not about who you are, where you are, what you have, or where you have been; you realize "I'm hooked. I'm not in control" for real. After all the years of lying to yourself and all the crazy excuses, you now admit where you really are. Most of these individuals that can tell you all about what state they're in, they can tell you how they got there and why. They will tell you what they are doing wrong, how they should go about making a change. They have the lines down just right; they know what to say to each person. They have been to the rehabs. They know the Word of God. They've been to the church house. They've talked to the preacher. They're caught up in the hard place. Back in the day, we would have said these individuals are "stuck on stupid" because they know the way but won't walk in it. They are in the hard place, that place of knowing where you really are and what to do, but are not able to do it. They're in danger of becoming what I call a lifer—never able to get clean, never able to be free, never able to move from where they are at, always on the continual yo-yo, the continual seesaw (Romans 7:14-24).

Sadly, this state can go on for years and years and years. Some people never get out. They just end up staying at the same place until they have an overdose and die or an overdose and live, but they are totally messed up in the head; they go in and out of jail, or worse, they get killed. They go through this madness day after day, week after week, month after month, year after year, and even decade after decade. Totally defeated, they stop living and only exist. They are truly the living dead. They are in the hard place, and when in the hard place, they know all the answers. Many have facilitated the drug classes while in AA and NA rehabs. They know, but not enough; they care, but not enough. They say, "One day I'll change, I'll get it together," but that day never comes. They let their appearance go; they don't care to keep themselves up any more. They stop caring about their health or what they eat, yet they know they need to change.

There are no words in the human vocabulary that can truly express what this time in the life of a junkie is really like. It is during this time that the person addicted to drugs loses homes, family, jobs, and real friends. They even lose self-respect. If this were a normal person under normal conditions, a man or woman would give or do whatever to save his family, friends, job, or home. The awareness of losing your child, having them taken by the state, putting them into a position of living hell, into a state of death. The awareness that your parents are old and could die—while you are still caught up. It would seem as though this would wake a person up and make them turn around, but it doesn't because they are "caught up." They are "stuck on stupid." Sort of reminds me of *Psalm 88*.

I remember ministering to a person in jail who was waiting to go to court again. He was already on parole when he caught the case that had landed him back in jail, and he was now facing a possible ten-year sentence or longer. He had been on drugs and in and out of jail for almost forty years. One could tell he had been a good-looking man at one time, but now he was old, sick, and frail. He wanted me and my wife to help him. He wanted to be probated into our ministry house instead of going to jail, but it was too late because the courts would not even give consideration to his request because of his record.

So here was this man who could tell me everything I came to tell him, and yet he sat so helpless and hopeless, facing the possibility that now at sixty-three, he would probably die in prison. He had wasted most of his life, and now he had such a faraway look in his eyes. I believe it was a look that was saying, "How could I have been so stupid to end up back here again?" This was the saddest day of ministry that I had experienced because I too sat there realizing that this old man who was now crying out would most likely die in jail, and there was nothing I could do to help him. He ended up with a sentence of fifteen years.

Yes, you want to be free. You wonder how and why you are at this place in your life. "How did it ever come to this?" You know it didn't happen overnight, but you want to be free. You want out. You are sick and tired of being sick and tired, and you want to be free. This is where I tell people that being "tired" is good, but it is not good enough, not if you want to be free. Tired does not count for much, but it is a start. When a person gets tired, they usually stop and get some rest and get back up again and continue on the path they were on. In addition to being tired, a person must become "broken" in order to be free. Psalms 51:10, 17 (KJV) says, "Create in me a clean heart, O God and renew a right spirit within me . . . The sacrifices of God are a broken spirit; a broken and a contrite heart, O God, thou wilt not despise." The essence of the word "contrite" means true repentance, true brokenness. It means to be humbled down, to collapse from one's own will into the will of God, to repent for real. To repent for real means to turn completely from sin and turn completely unto God.

Many people pray to be healed from drugs but still want a life of sin. They still want to be the whore, the lover, the dope man, the stickup man but just don't want to be addicted to drugs. They are just tired of not having the money to live a luxurious life of sin because all their money is going to the dope man. So they pray that God will heal them from their drugs, not realizing this would only make God an enabler to their sin life minus the drugs. They want God's help, but not God's remedy, not God's completeness, not God's holiness. God is waiting for us to come to the place of wanting, needing, and loving Him for the reasons God wants us to come to Him. He wants us broken and contrite (Psalms 37:4,23,24, Psalms 34:1-10, St. Matthew 11:29,30, St. John 1:12).

Yes, it is a good thing that now the addicted person is tired and they want to be free. They might go to various substance-abuse meetings or to the church. They might cry out to anyone that will listen, showing their sadness, but what we must realize is that this same individual who is tired can still go on for years under the control of drugs, believing that just being tired is enough, believing that being tired is the answer. Individuals try to make deals with God all the time. People want off the merry-go-round, but they want God on their terms. Many try to use God. They want God to get them off the drugs, but they don't want to follow God's Word, to keep God's commandments. Some people think that it wouldn't be so bad if they could be a functional addict, but now drugs are ruining everything. They want to eat, dress, and have a place to stay. They want a woman or man in their lives. They want a clean break in their mind, in their drug life, but not in their spirit (Matthew 15:7-9). WE HAVE TO REALLY "WANT IT," not just "I want it."

The battle cry that developed through my own personal experiences is "How bad do you want it, and what are you willing to give up to get it?" Until you want freedom more than you want drugs, you really don't want freedom. Until you want freedom more than any pleasures in sin, you really don't want freedom. You must come to the point in your life when you're willing to do more to get off drugs than what you were willing to do to get drugs. I came to the point in my life where I told God that if I had to live as a junkie, then I didn't want to live. All during my addiction, I stayed in church. Is not church supposed to be the hospital for the sick? I kept coming, and I kept praying for deliverance from my addiction until I got delivered for real.

Some people are tired of the hurt of using but not of getting high. I realized after many years of doing drug ministry that a part of what happened that enabled me to never be tempted again was the fact that I wasn't just tired of the hurt of using drugs, but I began to hate drugs. I don't know if I hated the high, but I hated the hurt so much, it didn't matter if I still desired the feelings that drugs gave me, because the hate of the hurt was one thousand times greater than the feelings from the high.

I have come to know that God is real and not just believe that God is real. I didn't simply believe in my heart because my mama raised me to believe in God, but I had a desire to know in my intellect that God was real. Once this happened, all the Bible verses I'd studied took on a new meaning, and I knew God for real. The Bible is a love story about Somebody that loved everybody so much that He gave His best, His all, even His only Son and continues to give and give. I found the Bible to be true and therefore found myself on my way to hell, just like the rock group Marilyn Manson's song says, "I'm on the highway to hell." I decided, oh no. I was not going to go there. I changed my song to "My Soul Has Been Anchored in the Lord" by Douglas Miller. It is hard to stop doing something that you don't hate but you rather still enjoy. It is so much easier not to do something that is devastating because you hate it.

Chapter Eight

The Art of Effective Ministry

Ephesians 4:11-16

Doing effective ministry is a calling. We must be led by God's Spirit at all times as we minister to these individuals. While I'm ministering, I'm praying for God's Spirit to intervene, and usually what I hear back from those I'm ministering to is this: "Man, God had to have told you that because that's just what I'm dealing with, just what I'm going through, that's just where I'm at." We cannot underestimate the power of the Holy Ghost while working in ministry. We must be wise as serpents while harmless as doves. Being harmless as doves does not mean that we are not sometimes in the face of the addict giving tough love because we must remember this adverse dysfunctional population that we are dealing with. These individuals who are now in the program have come out of a lifestyle where they are use to cheating, stealing, lying, and pimping their way into what they want. We must be a channel of love, patience, power, and challenge. Your job is to strive to get these individuals standing before you to see who it is that they should have become before they surrendered their life to drugs and a life a sin. Then don't leave them there, but now challenge them to strive by God's grace and mercy to become in life what God would have them to be at this time, because God still has a purpose and a plan for their lives. Some things that were supposedly dead God will restore and renew, and other things he will give you a new start in.

Let us deal with challenging for a moment. While ministering to men and women, I've learned that challenging them gives a lot of them something to prove. For example, I once knew a guy that I had to push him in order to get him to move toward healing and deliverance. At one point while he was in our ministry, I had to tell him that I would not accept the fact that this tough guy who was rough and tough in the world wasn't man enough to handle this one-year Christian ministry program (which is like army and Bible college together). Plain and simple, I asked him one day after he kept whining and crying about how hard it was to be in the program (basically because he could no longer do what he wanted to), "So what you gonna do? Punk out?" (I said it in the way that "punk out" is used in the street; it has nothing to do with sexuality). Basically, I was challenging him to man up. "You're tough enough to withstand all the hell you went through in jail and in the streets, but you gonna let this Christian program whip you?" Needless to say, this young man graduated with honors and is in college, working, and has accepted his call to the ministry.

Next, you must get these individuals to be truthful with themselves. Remember, they have been living a lie for so long, they sometimes start believing the lies that they live. Lying and not facing the truth becomes a part of them. When I was director of a ministry program in Chicago, we had a little saying called "Shakespeare 101—to thy own self be true." You cannot lie to God, and you must not lie to yourself. Facing the truth of who you have become will allow you the strength to become the new creation that God wants you to be. Getting these individuals to be truthful means getting them to face and deal with their root problems.

My former pastor, Reverend James C. Carpenter, taught me so much about being true to myself. I would not have made it if God had not put him in my life. One day while we were in his office, he read me like a book. He had listened to me and studied me for a season, making an effort to get to know the real me. As ministers, pastors, directors, we must learn to spend time studying those that God has put in our charge in order to bring out the best of what God wants in them. He realized that as a young man I had just overcome drugs and had a very rough street life. So this day in his office, while we were just sitting and talking about nothing, out of the blue and in a nonchalant voice and in a calm and kind manner, he said "Minister Houston, I believe you want to love God and others, and really you want to do things right in the ministry, but you are not who and what you say you are in the natural or in the spiritual. I can still see the freak in your eyes jerking off, and until you admit to yourself who and what you really are and where you're really at as opposed to who you say you are, you're not going to go anywhere spiritually or naturally." Then he just went back to talking about what we had been casually talking about. He had read me like an open book, and I was blown away. See, he knew because he himself had been an old hard-core drug addict, a pimp, and a street hustler off the cold mean streets of Chicago back in the fifties. He had gotten clean, went to college, and had become this awesome, mighty man of God who was a pastor's pastor.

Pastor Carpenter dealt with everyone in love, but everyone also knew he had a way of bringing what he was saying to you "straight" down the middle. He didn't hold back no punches. He told you straight, but always in love. He saw God's hand upon me for ministry, but he also saw that I had not really let go of all the things that bound me beyond drugs. I had not been sincere with myself yet, but his words caused me to actually go home, stay up all night, and be honest with myself and lay myself on God's operating table. I laid out all the good, the bad, and the ugly; and in truth, I realized there was very little good in me.

Because of what he did and the time he put into studying me, it taught me how to do effective ministry. I speak their language. I understand their pain and their game because I have lived so many various lifestyles in the streets, it's hard for them to bring nonsense to me. As we say in the streets, "Game recognizes game."

I have learned how to listen, allowed them to sometimes lead the conversation because engaging in normal conversations is a part of their healing. Here and now, they can set aside the game and take off the mask. Here they will be challenged with the truth of who they really are but with love and understanding. By doing this, they see and admit the truth of who they really are and where they really are at. I have learned how to befriend these individuals. Many times when I minister to them, we just engage in regular conversations about sports, politics, or whatever, giving them a sense of normalcy, opening up opportunities for relationship and trust. They need to know that every time they see me, I'm not going to just be talking about healing and deliverance, that I'm not just going to be preaching at them, but they must see me as someone who truly cares.

I have had both men and women say, "Man, this dude really cares. He really loves me." They had seen and felt my godly love for them while I've had some women who, because of where they are at in life, because they are searching for someone that would care about them for real and not just use them, misinterpret my reaching out to them. They are searching for real love, and because of this, they mistake my godly, sincere, affectionate love for a romantic love. When they realized that this was not the case, they got angry and fell away, but I won't stop loving the many because of the few that get it wrong.

The Christian ministry that I had gone through while it was great dealing with overcoming my drug issue never dealt with my other addiction, mainly my sexual addiction, my lust issues, in a way that would have really helped me. People like me need much more hands-on counseling and ministering. They taught the Word and told us to call on Jesus. I was not ignorant of the Word, having come from a long line of presiding elders and pastors and having been surrounded by many great pastors such as Reverend Leo Champion, Reverend James C. Carpenter, and Reverend Don Pagel, but just knowing the Word was not enough. I had no relationship with God. I needed to first be challenged. I needed to acknowledge my sexual addiction then needed to face that addiction and then to overcome it by application of the Word. I needed sexual healing just as bad as I had needed healing from my drug addiction.

The ministry that I was at gave me a lot in many areas, but nothing to heal me from the sexual addiction, and I desperately needed to be healed from my sexual issues. They would not even realistically address the issues. Yes, they taught that we were not supposed to have sex until we were married, but not from a realistic point of view. Remember, you are dealing with people who have used sex as a vice just as drugs was a vice. Sex had been a part of their addictive lifestyles. And now at this center, it was one thing not to be able to have sex, but they refused to let you even talk to a woman; or worse yet, you could not even look at a woman. And if you did, you were written up for lusting. In my opinion that was not reality, and that was not deliverance; and consequently, many brothers and sisters graduated the program and went out and fell quickly into fornication. We needed to learn how to interact with one another in a godly manner instead of for a whole year not being able to even look at a woman.

When the Lord healed me from drug addiction, I was totally healed from the moment He said it was over; but as healed as I am, if I were to ever use again, my chances of not relapsing do not exist. My chances of not becoming addicted is like the chances of me taking on both LeBron James and Kobe Bryant and winning. Yeah, right! I'm healed for real. I can go where I want to go and be around who I want to be around with, and I don't have to worry about using because there is no temptation, no desire. This was just as true in the beginning as it is almost twenty years later. People tell me I shouldn't say, "The devil ain't devil enough to make me go back to drugs." Well, he ain't! God won't do it, and the devil can't do it. Drugs is a dead man to me. When God healed me on September 26, 1993, the Holy Ghost said, "You'd better say it." And I've been saying it ever since. What I teach is when it's over, it's over, and it's over when God says it's over and you want it to be over. Therefore, before I got on the bus in 1993 to go to this Christian ministry, I was already healed from my drug addiction because God said it and because I wanted it, but God told me I needed to go and learn. This ministry by far has been one of the greatest blessings from God in my life. Yet I was still bound by my sexual addiction, and when I left this ministry, sex was what I gave into and battled for years until I was healed from it as I was from drugs. In 1993, concerning drugs, I was like the song that says, "I reached the turning point in my life," but I was not there yet with sex. It was not in my face. I was not challenged about my freak nature.

My prayer life tells the story. When I prayed, I usually prayed about both the drug and sex addiction, but if I prayed for an hour, fifty-nine minutes were spent on my drug addiction and one minute about the sexual addiction. Like I stated earlier, I left this ministry stronger, with more knowledge of the Word, delivered from my drug addiction, but I fell big time sexually because I was not yet healed; I was not yet delivered in this area because I wasn't serious about overcoming and being delivered from my lustful nature. I knew what the Word of God said about fornication, and I wanted to obey, but I just wasn't there yet. Drugs are not a natural habit, but sex is a God-given desire that we must learn to put into proper prospective according to God's Word. However, because I was not able to deal with these issues while at the ministry, I struggled with sexual addiction even while I was an elder.

From the time I was licensed in ministry, the sexual addiction had infected my subconscious; and even though I desired to live right, it was always there challenging me, and sometimes I fell. There were many times that I would flip a whole calendar without falling and then I would fall again the next year. I'd then get up, repent, and flip whole calendars for a season then fall again. I don't have the testimony of many that just walked away from sex after they started preaching and doing ministry. I had to crawl away. Remember how much trouble I had getting off drugs? Well, I had even more trouble with sex. This cycle continued until I was finally able to get true deliverance, but I had to wait until my change came.

I decided to talk about sexual addiction in this book because I know brothers and sisters who have given up because of their struggle with sexual addiction, but I want to encourage people to keep getting up until their mind is made up, and God will deliver them for real. It may have taken me a long time, and it was late in my life when this deliverance came, but thanks be to God, I finally got there. Remember the saying "Quitters never win and winners never quit."

> *The steps of a good man are order by the Lord, and He delights in his way. Though he fall, he shall not be utterly cast down, for the Lord upholds him with his hand. (Psalms 37:23-24)*

> *This poor man cried out, and the Lord heard him, and saved him out of all his troubles. (Psalms 34:6)*

I tell people all the time, "The reason you are not healed from drugs and from your dysfunctional lifestyle is because you are just not there yet." I wanted to be done with the drugs. I wanted to be healed, and God healed me. I did what was necessary on my part; we know God did His part, and the rest is history, but when it came to the sexual addiction, the fault lies in two areas. The first fault was with me because I was not yet willing or totally submissive to God. Second, I feel the ministry I was in did not deal with the issues. I tried to reach out to the pastors and counselors when I was in the Christian ministry center, but they did not respond to my cry. I was a minister in relapse with a drug addiction, but I knew that in order for my relationship with God to be complete, I had to deal with my root problems of which sexual lust was a major part. Whenever I would have a one-on-one meeting or conversation with one of the pastors, they would come in with their preconceived, prepared idea of what to talk about; they would come with their preconceived idea about what I needed and about what was going to help me.

In the beginning of this chapter, I talked about being led by the Holy Ghost. I would bring up my sex addiction, and they would reply, "Yes, and the Word says 'this'" or "The Word says such and such." They would give me a company line, so to speak, throw in a few verses, and then go back to their preprogrammed conversation, but many of us needed much more.

One of the things my first wife taught me was that when doing ministry, what and how you teach may work for some, but others may need it brought in another way, because what works for one does not always work for all. She taught me how to be versatile in ministry. Yes, I knew St. John 15:3—"You are already cleaned through the Word which I have spoken unto you"—but as it related to my sexual addiction, I was not there yet. This scripture did not have root in me yet with regard to my lust because I hadn't let go. I needed more. I needed to be challenged. I was not delivered. As a matter of fact, I was worse off because of some of their ministry's rules. The rules did not deal upfront with lust issues; neither did they teach us, as new men, how to deal with new women in the Lord. The way we operated during chapel and class was that the men sat on one side, and the women sat on the other side. You had to keep your eyes straight ahead. You'd better not look at a woman, smile at a woman, so you know you couldn't shake hands with a woman or, as I stated before, you were written up and accused of lusting. None of us in this ministry program were in preparation for priesthood. We were going to leave one day and return to the real world, and we needed discipline on how to have a real and godly relationship with the opposite sex. In my opinion, when ministering to ex-addicts, this approach is unacceptable and does not work as proven by the many who were delivered from drugs but fell into sexual condemnation after graduation.

 I benefited much spiritually from that Christian ministry program, but my experience helped to shape a different outlook toward total deliverance. At our ministry program, my wife and I are strong advocates of dealing first with root problems and strong advocates of teaching men and women in the program how to deal with and interact with one another in their new life. As a brother or sister in Christ, we should be able to approach, speak to, and shake hands with the opposite sex and be in control of our thoughts and emotions. We teach men and women who they are in Christ and how to respect one another in their new Godly nature. We teach them what kind of man or woman they should strive to become so one day they can marry the kind of Christian man or woman that is compatible to where God is taking them in life. Compatibility will help to generate a successful and happy relationship. When seeking for a mate, we teach that someone can be the right type but not the right one. One of the reasons is because some people are saved and really love the Lord but are not devoted to ministry, while others are saved and love the Lord and are wholeheartedly devoted to the work of the ministry. These two opposites cannot always survive in a relationship unless there is an understanding.

Listen, you can't just always take hard-core drug addicts and sex addicts out of the world and simply preach Jesus, Jesus, and more Jesus without doing any hands-on ministry that deals with underlying problems through one-on-one counseling and group sessions. You will fail in your mission because your process is flawed and not complete if you fail to do this. Actually, such ministries can create an unrealistic world perception by having men and women not to look at, communicate with, or socialize with one another for an entire year. Then after this time period, they are sent back into the world where they must mingle with the opposite sex daily and deal with the God-given natural sexual feelings they were created with. Should we think that we are just going to miraculously go back into society and not have these sexual desires anymore? It's unrealistic. We must teach men and women how to overcome impurity and to understand this wonderful mechanism called sexuality. We must teach them how to keep those desires under control and exercised as God intended. Don't ignore it. It won't go away.

Training Effective Ministers

I had been taught by Reverend James C. Carpenter Sr. that one of the functions of being a pastor was to understand that preaching on Sunday mornings was only about 20 percent of your duty. He also taught that one must be an effective administrator and an effective minister, able to relate to and reach out to hurting people during the week. We must see them where they are and challenge them to get to where God would have them to be. Reverend Carpenter always taught me that a good minister must be at the top of his game. He meant that a good minister should be a good listener who could then allow God to give them what to say instead of relying on your own knowledge and strength. He taught me how to study the Bible, apply the Bible, and then paraphrase it when ministering to others instead of just quoting it all the time. This way it does not make a person feel as though they are always being preached at but rather being ministered to, making the scriptures more effective as it becomes more personal to the person you are trying to reach.

Reverend Carpenter challenged me to look at and face my issues in this way. He challenged me to look at the how, when, where, and whys of my life without just quoting from the scriptures but by breaking it down and applying it. He made it relevant to my situation.

Thus, in my discipleship classes and my recovery group sessions, I've learned to give people hypothetic situations on the spur of the moment, situations of real life. Individuals have to get up in front of the class, pray for or witness to an individual who wants to get saved or who is in a devastating situation. The person doing the prayer or ministering only has a sixty-second window of opportunity. Then as a class, we critique and evaluate the performance of the individual for the purpose of education and training. This is their training grounds; this is where they learn to properly apply the scriptures and learn to listen to the voice of the Holy Spirit. This is where a person learns how to "stay in their lane" of ministry. Pastor Carpenter taught me that in order to be effective for the Lord, a person must learn what type of ministry God has called them to, and that is where you perfect your ministry. If you are a preacher and can't sing, then stick to preaching. If you are a pastor and not a prophet, then stick to pastoring. Do what God has called you to do, and do it well. Sometimes, learning to stay in your lane causes you to make hard decisions in order to follow God.

For example, the love, respect, and honor that I felt for Pastor Carpenter was that of a son toward a father. He indeed was my father in the Gospel. We were very close. When I graduated from the Christian ministry, he had expected me to come back to Milwaukee and work with him as he prepared me to take over the headship of the church upon his demise. I believe he knew his time was short. He was terminally ill, and he saw in me a call to pastoral leadership. He felt he had trained me and that I should be there. At the time, I really could not understand why I couldn't come back, but I felt in my spirit that it was not God's will. Believe me, it was not an easy decision because here I was having a church basically handed to me, but God said, "This is not the lane I want you in yet." It was the beginning of God leading me by my spirit. It was the beginning of God teaching me to walk in my lane. As much as I wanted to pastor, I had to tell this great man of God no. It broke his heart and mine too. He had nourished me in the ways of the Lord and brought me through my addiction and relapse. I remember him telling me once when I had relapsed back into drugs before my true deliverance that, "The only reason I don't sit you down right now is because I know it would break you, but if it happens again, I will put you out of this pulpit." His action and love forced me to see just how bad off I was, and I realized that I had to go then and get help.

He basically put me out without putting me out. His words caused me to leave within two weeks to get the help I needed. He knew I was using, but remember, he had studied me as he did all his ministers. He knew how I was, and he knew that his words and his love would cause me to leave. So for me to tell this father in the Gospel that I could not come back but was rather going to Chicago to work in street ministry and be an associate pastor with people I didn't even know was a bitter pill, but we both had to swallow it. I had peace in my spirit that I was hearing God. God was calling me to a specific type of ministry, to walk in a specific lane, to pastor a specific work. I would not have been successful or fulfilled just being a pastor of a church. I went to Chicago. Things were difficult in the beginning, but God removed my crutch; Pastor Carpenter passed away.

I had to endure and continue to believe God even when I didn't feel Him working year after year. I had to trust Him for the ministry vision that was in my head and in my heart. I was offered other opportunities to take over churches as pastor, but it was not my time yet. I allowed myself to get into bad circumstances by being in the wrong place for the wrong reasons; I got into a wrong situation (my first wife).

I went backward for so many years instead of going forward toward my destiny. I did not "guard my heart with all diligence" like the Bible instructs us to do. My first wife had to go and get help for her drug addiction at the same place I had gone, but she only stayed three days. When she came back, we ended up homeless. Here I go again—things got worse for seven long, long, hard years. But even though things were so very bad, I had to trust God for the vision in my heart, True Believers GROUP Outreach Ministries, just like I had to trust Him for my healing from drugs even when it seemed like healing would never come. Now instead of "how bad do you want the ministry," the question was would I hold on even though things were getting worse in my life again.

I am not going to talk about those seven years in detail. I can not. ReRe and I went through more hell in those seven years than we did with my addiction. Have you ever felt suspended between two places? That was where I was. I knew we were going through a crazy time, but I couldn't believe it. How had I gotten here again? There is so much I could teach from what happened in those seven years, but that is one nightmare I refuse to relive again. I feel like the man that ran an ad in the paper for his dog that was missing. The ad said, "Looking for my dog, he's missing one ear, is blind in one eye, has a paw missing on his back leg, and he answers to the name of Lucky."

I am so blessed that God brought my through time after time after time. So just like I believed God for my healing from addiction, the same determination was there to believe God about the specific area of ministry and pastoring he was calling me to. Now today I am walking in my lane, pastoring True Believers GROUP Outreach Ministries, helping the kind of people God wanted me to. All I can say is that, I was toast for those seven years. I don't really know how I got through all the craziness. It had to be Jesus that carried me through. Remember the poem "Footprints in the Sand." That was Jesus and me. Although TBGOM is in its infancy, we believe God will grow it to completion, one ministry home at a time.

Some pastors and churches have feeding programs and various other outreach ministries that are not as effective in reaching the lost as they could be. Too often, they allowed these individuals to run over them, to prey on the church because the saints have a good heart. If you really want to have an effective outreach program to reach this population, you must have someone within your church with vision and understanding of the people you're trying to reach. Addicts are smart, slick, and cunning. Many of them know how to give you the sob story that will melt your heart, but what they are really doing is telling you what they think you want to hear. They feed on your love, your compassion, and your Christlikeness. They walk away full, with money and other items, but with no challenge to change. In running rehabilitation and outreach ministries, a Christian has to sometimes be tough. We have to show tough love. The response of Pastor Thomas Barclay, my pastor in Chicago, to those that would come by the church seeking money would be, "Do you need some food, do you need a bus token, do you need some clothes? I'll give or help you get any of these things, but I don't give money."

I have to say this, that when it comes to doing ministry, there is a level that pastors get to that is beyond what could be called average. The heart and mind of the pastor becomes so focused that they really begin to just go all out in their effort to do ministry. It's like they have a spirit of ministry. They begin to do more than just pass out food or just meet needs. The mind set is more about doing ministry in the way they meet needs. They begin to set up all kinds of ministries in the church. The church begins to be open every day. They do so much for people that the people in the hood begin to love the church because of the love of God they see coming from the church. Pastor Barclay is on that level. Pastor Barclay made sure I learned from him everything he had to teach me from God before he let me leave to go out on my own. He made me stay longer than I wanted to and didn't care what I said because he was hearing from God and doing ministry. With him it was not about him or me, it was about God's ministry.

The addict and the dysfunctional must understand that while you are there to help them, you are not just a handout; your ministry is there to help those that are looking for a way out. You cannot just pass out food, quote a few verses, or just give a "praise the Lord." You must plant seeds; you must show friendship and create relationships in order for these individuals to leave with something that can take root and bring about a change in their lives for real.

True Believers GROUP Outreach Ministries is for people who really want Jesus. I'll feed you for a minute, house you for a minute, be patient with you for a minute, but if I see that you are just playing games, wanting a place to warm your ribs and don't want Jesus, then I'll pull you aside and let you know that perhaps this is not the place for you. I'll remind you of the conversation we had from the beginning because you cannot even get into the ministry house if you do not agree to acknowledge that this is a Christian ministry whose foundation is a personal relationship with Christ, which you must pursue in honesty. You can be so messed up on drugs that you don't know who you are, but if you want to change and agree to allow Jesus the opportunity to work in your life, then this is the place for you. Even so if my wife or I feel as though you are just playing, buying yourself some time, and using the program, we'll give you a warning with love and compassion. We'll even try to compel you to change, but if you don't get it together, then you are out the program. This is no game. It is a matter of life or death. I will pack you a lunch, pack up your clothes, and with tears in my eyes, have the staff drop you off at the nearest mission. They house people. We offer deliverance while housing. This is God's ministry. This is God's house, and I'd rather pastor an empty house before I allow people to run over and abuse the house of God. Everyone must do their part. I promise to do my part, and God will no doubt do His part. And every individual must do their part.

Effective Tactics

Many days I would go to our ministry house in Bloomington and get one of the fellas and say, "Come on, let's go for a walk." Other times in ministry, I would take someone off the streets in Chicago and take them to Denny's restaurant in the suburbs for coffee, getting them out of their environment and into another atmosphere where they could relax and talk. We would talk without the usual religious rhetoric. I would take them out their world of insanity and away from the "amen" and "hallelujah" for a moment just to talk. As ministers, we must not come across as though the only thing we're looking for is another opportunity to preach to someone. We must come across as good listeners, real and sincere, with it not being about us but really about the individual that is before us. Sometimes these individuals just need a friend, they just need a listening ear, and you have to become that living epistle, not with words but with actions, creating relationship. As ministers, we must also realize that we are dealing with people who were not just addicted to their substance of choice but to a lifestyle. So many of us get saved and become totally boring. We stop living although Jesus said He came to give us life and that more abundantly. These individuals are used to excitement. They are used to movement and action in their lives. What we must understand is that yes, we must be holy. No, we must not compromise, but we must be whole as well. We cannot become "dead men walking." In pastoring, there is the challenge of finding the lost soul, but the greater challenge is in keeping them.

While director of the ministry house in Chicago, one day I got all the "fellas." We loaded up a van, and we went to a bowling alley and pool hall. It was at a Brunswick bowling and billiards center, which happened to have a bar, but that didn't bother us. No, we didn't just go to a bar, but this was a family center where people came to bowl or play pool, and there happened to be bar on one side. We went into this particular facility, ordered our sodas, talked about life and the Word of God while those around us looked at and marveled at us. They knew we were different. We were saved, but we were still able to have a good time. Another time, we got some coolers, filled them with ice and sodas, got some meat to throw on the grill, and headed to the river. We stayed there from morning until evening, eating, fishing, talking, and having a good time. The men have often said to me, "Pastor Ray, we love dealing with you because you understand us. Man, you understand what we need." They knew that I was not stuck in tradition. I was not so stern that we could not let go and just have fun sometimes and enjoy life. For example, the fellas knew that if a play-off game happened to fall on regular group night, I might come in and say, "What's up somebody cook a meal, somebody order a pizza, or fire up the grill." We would pray, read a few verses, and then sit down, enjoy the game and fellowship. My being friends with the guys and being one of the brothers gave them greater respect for me, and during the times we had classes, I had their attention. They knew I loved them. They knew I felt them, and they knew I was serious when it was time to get down to the Word, and they greatly respected me for it. It's not me, but through the training I've had and the leading of the Spirit, I understand that a change in atmosphere can do wonders. I understand that you must teach these individuals how to live and have excitement in their lives the right way. Don't stop living, for life really only begins once you are in Christ.

As directors, pastors, ministers, and leaders to this population, we must provide entertainment and activities that will challenge the entire man to heal. It took me until I was in my forties to change and allow God to turn my life around. I wasted many valuable years because I would not give in to God. We must encourage those to whom we reach out to not to wait this long. It doesn't have to take them as long as it did for me if they would only yield and say yes to God. I was such a pookie always trying to do things my way. We must *challenge them to believe* "There is life after drugs - How bad do you want it?"

One of the unique things about True Believers GROUP Outreach Ministries is the traits that both my wife and I bring to the table. This book tells you all about me and my experience that makes me an effective leader, but Pastor Colleen is a powerful and unique individual within herself. She has a bachelor's degree in criminal justice and a masters in theology. She has over thirty years' experience in jail ministry, twelve of those as chaplain of the McLean County Jail. She understands the population that we deal with firsthand, having counseled, mentored, and been a court liaison for men and women during her tenure as chaplain. She was pastor and leader of a church for over thirty years and is a highly regarded motivational speaker and evangelist. She was doing in Bloomington what I was doing in Chicago. Only God could have looked down through time and put us together for such a time as this.

Let me close with this disclaimer. Remember the commercials that would come on with the stuntman doing something really crazy and a disclaimer would appear saying, "Dangerous, don't try this at home"? Well, I want to say don't get the wrong idea about anything in this book because anything that might sound glamorous or appealing about the life I led, the hell I went through during that time was a thousand times worse than what it sounds. There is a song by the Winans that has a line in it that says, "Millions didn't make it, but I was one of the ones that did." God just did me a favor, and favor ain't fair. So don't wait; now is the time. How bad do you want it?

In real preacher-like fashion, in my second (LOL) closing, I would like to thank Pastor William Bennett for all his financial support to True Believers GROUP Ministry. It has been such a big help. I would also be remiss if I didn't mention the following. I believe that God has used many dedicated individuals to help set free those of us struggling with addiction and other bondages. I would like to encourage all of you, if you don't have it, to immediately write the Potter's House and get the sermon (about 1994) *"The spell is broken"* by Bishop T. D. Jakes. It is an amazing, powerful, and inspirational message that will change your life. For the "pookies," the junkies, the addicted, the lost, and the lonely, this message touches every aspect of our lives while we're going through our craziness and gives us a word to be delivered. I believe this message will greatly move and inspire you as it did me. Please understand that with Christ, all things become new, and every spell, stronghold, or bondage in your life will fall. In my past arrogance, I wanted to believe that I was such a smooth brother and took great pride in that belief. Now I know that I was really one of the biggest TRICKS ever known to mankind. Today I'm ok to just be the "SQUARE FROM NOWHERE." There is no addiction, no root problem, no issue or circumstance that can stand up to the power of God. How bad do you want it?

Pastor Ray

Pastor Ray Houston's story is one of hope and life. A drug addict for over twenty-seven years, God allowed him to escape jail and dodge death; and at the height of his addiction, he raised a baby daughter as a single parent from the age of one year to be a successful college graduate and real estate agent who has never known the evilness of drugs or the lifestyle. Even as a junkie, he was able to give Cheriamor a mother's love and a father's protection. She became his inspiration to change, his inspiration to provide for her a college education so that she would never experience the things he had. Cheriamor has always lived a saved life, faithfully attending church with her dad from a child. She has maintained her purity as a young woman and is an effective and inspirational youth minister. Pastor Houston now lives in Bloomington, Illinois with his wife Pastor Colleen Bennett Houston where they co-pastor True Believers GROUP Outreach Ministries, a Christian drug-rehabilitation ministry, housing men (and in the near future, women) with substance abuse problems. Please feel free to visit our Web site at www.daddysgirlspromotions.com. For information about an opening at the center or to make a donation contact, Pastor Ray or Pastor Colleen at (708) 351-2581 or by writing True Believers GROUP, 1226 N. Hershey Road, Bloomington, IL 61704.

Index

A

Aaron, Hank, 15, 61
addiction
    drug, 32, 56, 69, 77
    sexual, 60-62, 86-90
addicts, 52-55, 77, 94
alcoholic, 66

B

Babe Ruth, 15, 61
Barclay, Thomas, 22, 93
Bennett, William A., 97
Bright, Bill, 19
Brown, James
    "Say It Loud—I'm Black and I'm Proud," 58
Brown, Jim, 15, 61
Bryant, Kobe, 17, 87

C

Carpenter, James C., Sr., 84-85, 90-92
Champion, Leo, 20-22, 26, 86
Charles, Ray, 22

Cheriamor (daughter)
    assistant to Reverend Pagel, 24
    college degree, 30
    joining of Demoiselle 2 Femme, 30
    kindergarten, 23
    real estate license, 30
    writing a church manual, 21
Circuit Court of Illinois, 73
cocaine, 46-47, 56
codependent, 72. *See also* enabler
control, 47, 54-57, 65, 69-70, 79
Crouch, Andre, 19

D

desire, 46-47, 54-57, 65, 90
dope house, 16
Douglas, Fredrick, 15, 61
Du Bois, W. E. B., 61

E

effective ministers, training of, 90
enabler, 20, 72, 74-75, 78

F

FBI, 32
freedom, 81-82

G

General Service Administration, 32
grace, 15, 49, 62-63, 73, 83
Green, Al, 19

H

Holy Ghost, 48, 63, 83, 87
Houston, Ray
  as an addict, 15-16, 19, 81
  apprenticeship, 15
  being sexually active, 61-62
  as a businessman, 15
  evilness, hatefulness, and loneliness, 11-12
  getting broke, 12
  in jail, 14
  with Marie, 13, 18
  meeting his first wife, 73
  as a minister, 32, 52, 89
  molested, 60
  painting job, 32
  reasons for writing this book, 31-33
  relationship with his father, 77
  relationship with his mother, 29
  seeking God, 18-19
  as a single parent, 11-13, 27-28

I

insanity, 34

J

Jakes, T. D.
  "Spell is broken," 97
James, LeBron, 17, 87

K

King, Martin Luther, Jr., 15, 60-61

L

lifer, 79
Living Waters Ministry, 20-21
lust, 88

M

Mack, The, 58
Malcolm X, 15, 61
Marie (lover), 13-17
Married . . . with Children, 26
Mattie (sister), 10, 16, 19-20, 25, 27
mercy. *See* grace
Mighty Clouds of Joy, 19
Milwaukee, 9, 58, 64
ministering tactics, effective, 94
molestation, 60

N

Nee, Watchman, 19
Neoccesha (daughter), 12, 25-28
Nicky (son), 12, 25-28

O

Obama, Barack, 32

P

Pagel, Don, 21-26, 86
Pastor Colleen, 96
peer pressure, 56, 60-62, 65-66
pimp, 22, 56, 58, 68, 70-71
poverty, 60
pride, 56, 60
prodigal son, 29, 70
Psalm 88, 18, 80

S

Satan, 56, 63-65, 68-70
"Say It Loud—I'm Black and I'm Proud" (Brown), 58
self-esteem, 56, 64, 80
sexual immorality, 56, 60, 64
Shaft, 58
Simpsons, The, 26
smoke house, 16
"Spell is broken" (Jakes), 97
Super Fly, 58
Sweet Sweetback Song, 58

T

True Believers GROUP Outreach Ministries, 92, 93-94, 96-97

W

Washington, Booker T., 61
witchcraft, 55, 68
Word of God, 19, 62, 87

www.ingramcontent.com/pod-product-compliance
Lightning Source LLC
Chambersburg PA
CBHW031258290426
44109CB00012B/632